Make
Disciples
That Make
Disciples

Tim
Garland

MAKE DISCIPLES THAT MAKE DISCIPLES
A Six-Month How-To Book on Multiplying Disciples

By Tim Garland
© 2019 Tim Garland
All Rights Reserved.
ISBN 978-1-7343519-2-7

Editor: Michelle Segrest, Navigate Content, Inc.
Cover Design: Joseph DiGirolamo

DISCLAIMER

TABLE OF CONTENTS

INTRODUCTION 9
MAKE DISCIPLES OF ALL NATIONS   *9*

I DISCIPLESHIP - WHAT IS IT? HOW DO WE DO IT?   **13**
CHAPTER 1 13
WHAT IS DISCIPLESHIP?   *13*

CHAPTER 2 19
WHY DISCIPLESHIP?   *19*
Why Discipleship?   21

CHAPTER 3 25
HOW DOES DISCIPLESHIP WORK?   *25*

CHAPTER 4 29
WHO DO I DISCIPLE?   *29*

CHAPTER 5 35
WHAT DO I DO WITH THE DISCIPLE?   *35*
The Three Questions   36
The Three Cs   37

CHAPTER 6 41
IN WHICH AREAS DO I NEED TO TRAIN THE DISCIPLE?   *41*

CHAPTER 7 45
WHY ISN'T EVERYONE A DISCIPLER?   *45*

II DISCIPLESHIP - WHAT ARE WE TO BELIEVE?   **53**
CHAPTER 8 53
THE WORD OF GOD   *53*
The Bibliographical Test   55
The Internal Evidence Test   56
The External Evidence Test   60
The Bible is God-Breathed and Useful   63
How Can We Understand What *The Bible* Says?   66
MORE VERSES FOR FURTHER STUDY AND REFLECTION   74

CHAPTER 9 75
THE GOSPEL—THE LIFE, DEATH, BURIAL, AND RESURRECTION   *75*

What Is The Gospel? 77
What Are the Implications of The Gospel? 82
The Greatest Need for Everyone is The Gospel 87
How Can We Remain Gospel Centered? 88
MORE VERSES FOR STUDY AND REFLECTION 91

CHAPTER 10 93
GRACE—UNMERITED FAVOR TO THOSE WHO DESERVE WRATH 93
Common Grace vs. Specific Grace 93
Why Is Grace Needed? 97
MORE VERSES FOR STUDY AND REFLECTION 104

CHAPTER 11 105
LORDSHIP OF JESUS CHRIST 105
Can Jesus Be Your Savior and Not Your Lord? 105
He Is LORD. Is He Your Lord? 111
What Does It Look Like for Us to Acknowledge Him as Lord? 112
MORE VERSES FOR FURTHER STUDY AND REFLECTION 118

CHAPTER 12 119
ASSURANCE 119
What Can Take Away Your Salvation? 125
We Cannot Come to Christ Unless He Draws Us 127
MORE VERSES FOR FURTHER STUDY AND REFLECTION 130

CHAPTER 13 131
POSITION IN CHRIST 131
Who Were We? 131
Who Are We Now? 133
MORE VERSES FOR FURTHER STUDY AND REFLECTION 142

CHAPTER 14 143
FAITH 143
What Is Faith? 144
How Do We Get Faith? 146
Saving Faith and Sustaining Faith 147
How Do We Live a Life of Faith? 152
MORE VERSES FOR STUDY AND REFLECTION 153

III DISCIPLESHIP - WHAT ARE WE TO DO?   **155**
CHAPTER 15 155
PRAYER   *155*
What Is Prayer?   156
When Do We Pray?   156
How To Pray?   160
Why Pray?   163
MORE VERSES FOR FURTHER STUDY AND REFLECTION   166

CHAPTER 16 167
BIBLE STUDY   *167*
Observation   168
Interpretation   169
Application   171
Gospel   172
How to Have a Bible Study Plan   174
How Do I Begin?   176
MORE VERSES FOR FURTHER STUDY AND REFLECTION   177

CHAPTER 17 179
CHURCH   *179*
What Should Happen In The Church?   180
The Great Commission of the Church   182
Sacraments of the Lord's Supper and Baptism   185
The Church Leadership   187
You and The Church   192
MORE VERSES FOR FURTHER STUDY AND REFLECTION   195

CHAPTER 18 197
FELLOWSHIP   *197*
MORE VERSES FOR FURTHER STUDY AND REFLECTION   206

CHAPTER 19 207
EVANGELISM   *207*
How Do We Earn the Right to Speak Into People's Lives?   210
How Does Anyone Have Time for Evangelism?   212
What Do I Say?   214
MORE VERSES FOR FURTHER STUDY AND REFLECTION   216

CHAPTER 20 217
DISCIPLESHIP MEETINGS 217
Get to know those with whom you are discipling 219
MORE VERSES FOR FURTHER STUDY AND REFLECTION 222

CHAPTER 21 223
LIFE ON LIFE 223
MORE VERSES FOR FURTHER STUDY AND REFLECTION 231

IV DISCIPLESHIP - HOW ARE WE TO LEAD? **233**
CHAPTER 22 233
LEADERSHIP 233
Are You A Leader? 235
MORE VERSES FOR STUDY AND REFLECTION 238

CHAPTER 23 239
LIFE MANAGEMENT 239
MORE VERSES FOR FURTHER STUDY AND REFLECTION 254

CHAPTER 24 255
GOAL ACHIEVING 255
The Secular/ Sacred Divide 257
Goal Achieving Begins with Knowing our Roles 259
Goal Setting/ Achieving 263
MORE VERSES FOR FURTHER STUDY AND REFLECTION 268

CHAPTER 25 269
TALENTS 269
Temperament 273
Affections 275
Life Experiences 276
Education 277
Need 279
Training 280
Spiritual Gifts 281
MORE VERSES FOR FURTHER STUDY AND REFLECTION 284

CHAPTER 26 285
VALUES-VISION-RESOLUTIONS 285
Values 285

Vision   288

Resolutions   297

MORE VERSES FOR FURTHER STUDY AND REFLECTION   301

CHAPTER 27 303

LIFE MISSION   303

Calling   310

MORE VERSES FOR FURTHER STUDY AND REFLECTION   312

CHAPTER 28 313

TEAM   313

Team Building   316

Church/ Nonprofit/ Collective/ Partnering/ Merging   317

MORE VERSES FOR FURTHER STUDY AND REFLECTION   320

About the Author   323

TIM GARLAND   323

Acknowledgments   325

MAKE DISCIPLES OF ALL NATIONS

> *"All authority in heaven and earth has been given me, therefore, go and make disciples of all nations, baptizing them in the name of the Father, the Son and the Holy Spirit and teaching them to obey all I have commanded you. And surely I am with you always to the very end of the age."*
> *Matthew 28:18-20*

These are the last words of Jesus Christ before he ascended to Heaven. This is his final mandate to the church. The "Great Commission," therefore, the mission of the church. The amazing truth in most countries around the world in the church is that it is more often the "Great Omission."

The church does great things in the name of Jesus— feed the hungry, clothe the naked, put roofs over the heads of the homeless, fight for civil rights, provide for the needs of children, and many more good deeds. These acts are living out the hands and feet of Jesus to a lost world, meeting these immediate needs. These acts Glorify God, however, are they fulfilling the 'great commission.'

I believe these acts not only Glorify God, but they are necessary to communicate that we love people. This love for people opens the doors into their lives so that we can walk through to proclaim the Gospel of Jesus Christ to them, disciple them, train them to evangelize, and train others for generations after generations. The church is still very active in being the hands and feet of Jesus around the world, yet it often stops short of walking through the door that they have worked so hard to open. We must live out the mandate that God has given us through the last words of Jesus—**Go and Make Disciples of all Nations!**

"What is discipleship and what is Jesus calling us to in Matthew 28:18 20? Is this a command, or a suggestion? Does it mean we are just to evangelize and let people find faith on their own, or does this mean we are to lead others and teach the precepts of the Scriptures and the character of our Lord?

Does it require obedience and action on our part, or are we disciples just by being a Christian and being in a church on Sundays?

The passage at the end of Matthew's Gospel is what it is called the 'Great Commission.' This is also the great failure of the church! This is the main call to the church from our Lord and Savior, and it is the one thing most churches do not do at all! This is the main reason for a church to exist, yet can you name one church that actually teaches people the basics of the faith and then moves them deeper in to the precepts of His love and Word through all seasons of life?

If discipleship is mostly absent from our churches, then most Christians will not understand how to live out their faith. They will not be able to handle problems, witness, share their faith, or grow effectively spiritually because no one is modeling or showing them the way! Some churches do a great job with evangelism, but once the people come in, they are stored in the pews. Where is discipleship?

What is it? Is the back door of the church as big as the front door?"

Dr. Richard J. Krejcir (Krejcir, 2002)

This book was written primarily as a means of teaching how to make disciples that make disciples. How do we fulfill the great commission?

Should the great commission be the mission of the church? Is it in mine? Why not?

This book was designed with small same gender groups in mind. After the first 7 chapters explaining what discipleship is and how to do it, each chapter thereafter fills in the content of discipleship. Chapters 8-28 each have seven verses listed at the end of the chapter for further study on the topic of the chapter. To best utilize this book as a training manual, I advise each person to use those seven verses as their personal time alone with God verse of the day. If you followed the plan of each verse at the end of the chapter as daily bible study and read one chapter per week then this book would cover approximately 6 months of training.

My hope is that each person who takes this training manual serious would then take others through the same training... that we would make disciples that make disciples.

CHAPTER 1

WHAT IS DISCIPLESHIP?

> *"And the things you've heard me say in the presence of many witnesses, entrust to reliable men who will also be qualified to teach others."*
> *II Timothy 2:2*

Discipleship is a word that is thrown around in churches all the time. For many churches, discipleship training equates to some bible study classes on Sunday or Wednesday night. At one church, I decided to teach a Discipleship Training Class, and I called it "Discipleship." I thought that new members would learn what Discipleship means before registering for Discipleship Training Classes. I was very wrong.

In a church with about 800 in average attendance, I had only two to attend. One was someone I had discipled years earlier, and the other had been a former missionary who also had experience in discipleship. What I have learned is that most Christians are familiar with the word discipleship, but not many truly understand its process.

This is a good definition of Discipleship:

> "Discipling others is the process by which a Christian with a life worth emulating commits himself for an extended period of time to a few individuals who have been won to Christ, the purpose being to aid and guide their growth to maturity and equip them to reproduce themselves in a third spiritual generation."
>
> Discipleship as defined by Allen Hadidian, in his book, "Discipleship – Helping Other Christians Grow" (Hadidian, 1987)

In viewing the life of Jesus Christ there are many amazing events that one could find. One very important characteristic of Jesus' life that is often overlooked is His ministry. Jesus Christ's life was spent doing the will of the Heavenly Father.

> "There was nothing haphazard about his life, not an idle word. He was on business for God."
>
> Robert E. Coleman, The Master Plan of Evangelism (Coleman, 2010)

A very important part of His life that is not noted enough is that He devoted His life to the Kings' business, and also to the King's people. Jesus spent the last three years of His life performing miracles, preaching, teaching, healing, and walking on water. And He spent the entire time discipling men. One of the largest examples that Jesus left us was how His Father planned on reaching the world with the Good News of Jesus Christ's death, burial, and resurrection was through us. God's method of communication was men.

> *"One cannot examine the ministry of the Lord Jesus without seeing the emphasis He placed on discipling. . . From the very beginning, Christ's strategy of ministry centered on His men. He was always with them—teaching them, training them, encouraging them, rebuking them, and working His ministry in front of them. They became the main focus of His ministry."*
> *Allen Hadidian (Hadidian, 1987)*

Discipleship is when a mature Christian helps an immature Christian become mature. Then the mature Christian equips the growing Christian to reproduce himself into a third spiritual generation.

"And the things you have heard me say in the presence of many witnesses entrust to reliable men who will also be qualified to teach others. Paul to Timothy to reliable men to others."
II Timothy 2:2

Four spiritual generations are expressed in II Timothy by Paul. He does not want the training to stop with Timothy. Paul had given his life away to train Timothy. He knew that is how Jesus' strategy worked. He had to reproduce himself. He couldn't. He wouldn't let what God had been doing through him stop when he was gone.

Too few ministry leaders understand this principle of reproducing themselves. I've seen too many ministries dissolve because one leader left. These were leaders who didn't take the time to reproduce themselves. I learned through a college ministry called Campus Outreach that it would be fatal to the ministry if we didn't spiritually reproduce.

When I was a college student, I was given the opportunity to be the campus director for Campus Outreach Ministry. There was no full-time staff, and the Area Director devoted time to develop me for that role.

As I was approaching graduation, I noticed that many of the men I had discipled had already graduated ahead of me. This was a cost of cramming a four-year degree into six years. I saw the fate of the ministry at my campus have to begin again at square one. I devoted my last year and a portion of the year after graduating to discipling men.

The result was that those five men had a larger impact on my fraternity and campus than I could ever have had on my own. The Campus Outreach Ministry then sent a team of full-time staff to grow the ministry even larger, and of course, each one with a focus on discipleship. The longevity of a ministry depends upon the leaders' ability to reproduce themselves.

Another experience I had with discipleship was with a faithful Christian brother, Trace Donahoo. Trace was a missionary in England, who now serves as a Church Planter. He is a man that I spent so many years with in a discipleship relationship that truly anything I can accomplish in ministry he can also accomplish. And he caught the same vision of duplicating his life and training to others for the rest of his life. The result is that he has men he has discipled who have discipled men who are discipling men who could all probably accomplish anything I can accomplish in ministry, as well. The process of discipleship develops spiritual leaders for the next generations.

Discipleship is truly a life-on-life or heart-on-heart ministry that changes lives right in front of your eyes. It is not a ministry with fast results. It does not recruit the lazy or mediocre. It isn't for everyone. But everyone can do it.

CHAPTER 2

WHY DISCIPLESHIP?

The Reason for discipleship is that there are many converts to Christianity every year, but as the years pass, reproduction is not evident in each believer.

> *"Emotion is no substitute for action, action is no substitute for production,"— thus, he pointed out the difference between pew sitting and evangelism. Later he added the clause, `. . . And production is not substitute for reproduction; summarizing the difference between evangelism and disciple-making."*
> *Dawson Trotman*

Robert Foster in the book, *The Navigator,* (Foster, 1983, 2012) noted that if one man tries to bring the world to Christ it just isn't possible, but if the first man converted is trained and active in reaching the world for Christ, then that is when you have a growing ministry. Is it really possible? I am going to show you that it is more than possible. It is probable.

There is a huge difference between an evangelist and a discipler. The difference is that a discipler is also an evangelist, but simply because one shares the Gospel does not mean that he is a discipler.

> *"We loved you so much that*
> *we were delighted to share with you*
> *not only the gospel of God, But our*
> *lives as well, because you had*
> *become so dear to us."*
> *I Thessalonians 2:8*

Discipleship is truly sharing your life with someone. These men were not simply sharing the Gospel and leaving newborn children of God out for the lion to devour.

> *". . . The devil prowls around*
> *like a roaring lion, looking for*
> *someone to devour."*
> *I Peter 5:9b*

No, they were training men to resist the devil, to stand firm, and to live a life worthy of the Gospel of Jesus Christ.

WHY DISCIPLESHIP?

Discipleship teaches and trains new converts how to grow in their relationship with God. It gives them a mentor to walk them through the process so that they can stand firm, be strong and courageous, and that the fruit of their new life will remain.

> ". . . And appointed you to go
> and bear fruit that will last."
> John 15:16b

The results are that each believer who gets trained in discipleship has the best chance of continuing to grow in their faith. This provides the greatest opportunity to stay the course for a lifetime.

Also, the long-term number results are much greater. In the following illustration used by Allen Hadidian in the book *Discipleship-Helping Other Christians Grow* (Hadidian, 1987), shows these results. If an evangelist reaches 1,000 people with the Gospel of Jesus Christ per day, every day of the year, then he would reach 365,000 people per year. If a discipler reaches two people and trains them how to reproduce into another person each year while the discipler does the same then the results, while slower, will eventually exceed that of the evangelist who reaches even 365,000 per year.

In addition, those the discipler reaches are trained men and women of God rather than new converts. The results are expressed in the following table:

Years	Evangelist	Discipler
1	365,000	2
2	730,000	4
10	3,650,000	1,024
19	6,935,000	524,288
20	7,300,000	1,048,576
25	9,125,000	33,554,000
26	9,490,000	67,108,864
27	9,855,000	134,217,728
184	67,160,000	

Four billion people would be reached by the discipler in 32 years, while it would take an evangelist 10,960 years to reach the same amount of people with an average of 1,000 converts per day. These numbers do not express the fact that the discipler will be sharing the Gospel along the way with the people he or she comes into contact with, not including the ones being discipled. Those converts are not included in the numbers above. What is probably more possible for most of us is leading 1,000 people to Christ per day or discipling two people per year. The results are obvious. Why aren't more people discipling others? Why haven't we all been trained to do this already?

If you were offered one million dollars or the option of having a penny doubled every day and then that money doubled the next day every day for 30 days, which would you choose? Imagine with me that it is Day 2, and you only have 2 cents. On Day 3 you have 4 cents, on Day 5 you have 8 cents, and so forth. On Day 15 you have about $300 and that is when most people quit and complain that it's just too much work. It takes too long to see the results. I'm just not willing to put in the time it takes to catch up. After 30 days, the penny would be worth $5,368,712.34. Which way is wiser? Evangelist verses Discipler…which way is wiser?

Wisdom isn't always easier, but the results are always best.

CHAPTER 3

HOW DOES DISCIPLESHIP WORK?

Discipleship begins with a Christian with a life worth emulating—one who has faithfully been walking with Jesus Christ in the details of their life. The length of time is not as important as the quality of time displayed in consistency. The Christian who desires to train others must have been trained in the basics of walking with God. These basics are expressed in detail in the latter chapters of this book. Some examples are: how to have a quiet time with God on a daily basis, scripture memory, a view of God, evangelism, prayer, the church, and many others.

Once the believer has established the basics of Christianity, and the discipler sees consistency in the life of the discipled, one can move into the equipping stage. This stage consists of truly beginning to take the disciple with you in ministry and showing them the way. They must be with you to see you living out the ministry in front of them. They must see you do the things you are trying to train them how to do. You can only take them where you have gone or are presently going. You cannot take them further than you are willing to go.

However, God can take them much further as they follow Him through you. Remember, our goal is that they follow God for a lifetime. We are aiding and guiding that growth so that they will follow Him for a lifetime. In this role of leadership, we must also be careful, because they will catch our negative traits, as well. We must constantly remind them that we are fallible, and they must follow Christ in us. We become their teacher, not their master. Jesus Christ is their master. We are simply teaching them the best ways we have seen in following our Master so that they can also succeed in following Him.

When you discover that they are successfully following Christ in all areas, you must cast vision for them to reproduce themselves into others so that the process continues on and on. They can see the impact that you have made in their life, and most will automatically want to impact others. They can catch the vision for multiplying their lives through others for a lifetime, so that Jesus Christ can be known throughout the world. Page 16 has a road map of this process of discipleship from non-believer through exported disciple. On page 16 notice that it has very clear stages and steps to take at each stage.

Also, it is described how to recognize where the person is in their journey. You may also notice where you are and become more aware of the potential growth needs in your own life. The following map was written to assist Campus Outreach Ministry while I was in college. It may come from some Navigators Ministry documents or someone involved with one of the aforementioned ministries may have developed this map as a tool for discipleship. I received it in college through Campus Outreach. I pass it on to you as a tool. There are several tools out there. Maybe you could enhance this tool to meet your ministry needs.

The Discipling Map on the next page clearly describes five stages in a person's spiritual journey. The stages begin with being a non-Christian and end with being a mobilized disciple. Each stage has a defined description that allows one to discover where the person is on that journey.

The bold print word after the circle describes the step the discipler must take to move the person to the next stage of their journey. This, again, is only a tool. Please utilize the principles it describes to meet the needs of your personal ministry or discipleship relationship. Many of the steps included in this map will be explained in greater detail later in the following chapters.

Discipling Map

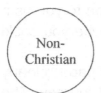

Non-Christian

EVANGELIZE

Moldable Disciple

ESTABLISH

Maturing Disciple

EQUIP

Multiplying Disciple

EXPORT

Mobilized Disciple

Evangelize a Non-Christian by:
1. Build Report with the non-believer
2. Identify where they are in their spiritual interest
3. Remove potential barriers
4. Share the Gospel, bringing them to a decision point
5. Effectively follow-up a person who repents and believes

Marks of a Moldable Disciple:
1. Has made a clear decision to repent and believe
2. Has assurance of salvation
3. Has a dislike of sin
4. Has a desire for God's Word

Establish a Moldable Disciple by:
1. Aiding their growth in a proper relationship with God
2. Aiding their growth in a proper relationship with Self
3. Aiding their growth in a proper relationship with Others

Marks of a Maturing Disciple:
1. Are building right relationships with God, self and others
2. Are growing in spiritual disciplines (means of Grace)
3. Involved in personal ministry (evangelism, Bible study)
4. Growing to model Christ in character, values and vision

Equip a Maturing Disciple to Multiply by:
1. Training them to evangelize and establish others
2. Leading them in their personal ministry
3. Help them to discern God's Call in their life
4. Assist them in the development of a personal vision

Marks of a Multiplying Disciple:
1. Growing deeper and consistent in their walk with Christ
2. Active in evangelism and discipling others
3. Committed life to follow Christ in discipleship

Export a Multiplying Disciple by:
1. Help develop them to servant/lead in ministry
2. Connect them with ministry that utilizes their TALENTS
3. Help them develop a personal life mission statement

Marks of a Mobilized Disciple:
1. Evangelizing and Discipling
2. Using their TALENTS in the context of the Local Church
3. Ordering their life in light of God's calling

28

CHAPTER 4

WHO DO I DISCIPLE?

Jesus wasn't looking for men who were the Kings, rulers, political leaders, salesmen, or the like. He did not have certain professions in mind, temperaments, personalities, or leadership abilities. He was looking for faithful, available, and teachable men. He didn't look for men of prestige, nor of great ability. He sought men of availability. He didn't search for the extraordinary. He sought the ordinary.

You are looking for a moldable disciple from the chart on the previous page. Also, there may be someone who falls into one of the other categories with whom you could assist the rest of the way. You are looking for someone who is willing to reproduce when they are mature. This process of discipleship is an investment with a lifetime of return.

I was on staff at a church in which I challenged seven men to discipleship. I then concluded by saying that they couldn't collectively say yes to the commitment. I told them that they must each individually come to me and convince me that they are ready for the commitment to the process for a lifetime. I didn't want them to take the process lightly. It is serious business. Lives are truly at stake.

Four of those men individually came to me and were ready. Within about eight months, two of them were already leading others in discipleship. It is extremely important to understand that your readiness is not determined by time, but by growth.

If you cannot find anyone to disciple, share your faith with everyone the Holy Spirit leads you toward and pray that the Holy Spirit would prepare someone for you to disciple. He is faithful, and you should remember that perhaps the person or people God has for you are not ready yet. While you are growing in your personal relationship with Jesus Christ. He can use you to bring someone into faith in Him, and you can disciple that person.

If we share the Gospel of our Lord Jesus Christ often enough the problem will not be having faithful, available, and teachable men to disciple, the problem will be having enough trained leaders to disciple the new converts.

Recognize in the last chapter about the process. It begins with those who are not yet believers. Anyone who is willing to spend time meeting with you is a potential discipler. My own experience was with a man who invested time for eight weeks in a Bible Study that was teaching me topically the basics of Christianity. This happened before I was a Christian.

Look for faithful men or women. Someone who will show up to meet with you on a regular basis defines faithful in this context. Don't set the bar too high until they are being established in the basics and the Holy Spirit is at work in their life. Do not forget too quickly what you were like in your Christian infancy. Expect faithful attendance to meetings. Beyond that, remember where they are in their growth process and that you are leading them forward. This requires time and patience on your part.

Look for available men or women. If there truly is no time in their week to meet with you after several attempts, then you should discuss again with them the seriousness of the commitment and ask if they can commit to a weekly meeting with you. If they cannot commit to a weekly meeting, then they are not available to be trained.

Look for teachable men or women. If they are filled with pride and think they already know everything, they may not be teachable. Have a serious conversation about the importance of the training so that they can train others. They must be a learner to be teachable.

How do we find faithful, available, and teachable men or women? Depending on your gender, men should disciple men, and women should disciple women.

We must be active in people's lives around us. We must have contact to have an impact. We should know our neighbors, co-workers, and other people whose paths we cross every day. I have developed a habit of eating at the same place, buying gas at the same place, going into the bank to make a deposit—all so that I can have multiple touches in the same people's lives.

For example, as I write this, I am eating breakfast with my usual waitress, and having a great conversation with her. I am also waiting to have a meeting at my bank with another person with whom I have an ongoing friendship because I regularly meet with him. Neither of these two people this morning are Christians yet.

I invest my time into making contacts with people intentionally for the purpose of loving them well in hopes that I can share the Gospel with them and that they will eventually become Christians. I call it living with the Gospel intentionality. You will read more about this in Chapter 19 about Evangelism.

This lifestyle allows me the access to a number of people with whom to speak about discipleship. If we practice this model, we will always have people we are either evangelizing or discipling.

Where do we find the people to disciple? You probably already know them or at least see them every day. If we have Gospel intentionality in our lives, then the future disciple makers will literally be all around us.

CHAPTER 5

WHAT DO I DO WITH THE DISCIPLE?

Many people think that if they meet the person occasionally and pass on information to them then they have done their job discipling them. Review the definition used in the first part of this chapter.

> *"... The purpose being to aid and guide their growth to maturity and equip them to reproduce themselves in a third spiritual generation."*

In the book, *The Master Plan of Evangelism*, (Coleman, 2010) Robert E. Coleman wrote,

> *"He actually spent more time with His disciples than with everybody else in the world put together. He ate with them, slept with them, and talked with them for the most part of His entire active ministry."*

The discipler must devote his life for an extended period of time to assist, train, uplift, rebuke, aid, and guide them in all aspects of their desire to have a growing relationship with Jesus Christ.

If you are getting overwhelmed at this point, don't worry. I did, too. One of my mentors advised me that if I will simplify the process by adding a few systems to what I do with my disciples, it can make it easier to know my next steps. One of these systems is to pray, think, love, and serve my disciples.

THE THREE QUESTIONS

Another system I like to use is a goal-setting system of looking at where you are trying to take the disciple. With all of our life's goals there should be three basic steps. The first step is to decide where you want to go. What is the next desired goal of training or understanding?

The second step is to look at where the disciple is right now. Utilize the Map on page 16 for this exercise, as well as the final system in this section.

The third step is to determine the next step to get them where they are going. To simplify this system, think about a Geographical Positioning System (GPS). The first step is to type in the address of where you want to go, the second is the device connects with satellites to determine where you are, the last step is to press GO. The device gives you each next step along the process.

- Where am I taking my disciple(s)?
- Where is my disciple in their growth right now?
- What is the next step in the training process?

THE THREE CS

Conviction, competence, and consistency are the topics of the next system.

Conviction is built by the Holy Spirit through the Word of God. Competence is achieved by training and teaching the disciple how to do something. Consistency is built through accountability for set goals.

People often try to build conviction in other people by convincing them of a truth. The truth is that all they have done is sold them on a good idea. The difference between a good idea and a conviction is that a good idea is something you hold, and a conviction is in the hands of God, and it holds you.

Conviction is God's hold on your life in a certain area through the guidance and power of the Holy Spirit. When you are trying to help a Christian grow in their relationship with God in a specific area or struggle, take them to the Word of God. Also, if we want the Holy Spirit to go to work in their inner being, we must pray that the Holy Spirit will convict their heart in that area.

Conviction may take time, but believe me, you want your disciple to develop convictions of their own. If they only follow because you do, they will likely quit when you are no longer around. You want them to drink from the fountain, and not only from your bowl. When God works in their soul by the power of the Holy Spirit through the truth of His Word to build conviction in a Christian's life it holds them.

Advise, direct, instruct, but do not try to be the Holy Spirit. He will do His part every time and on time. We must focus on our part of teaching and training them in the truth, while trusting God through prayer to instill the truths into their lives.

Other than prayer, time, love, and thinking for our disciples, the largest role the discipler plays in the discipleship process is to train them. The training needs to happen on a weekly basis. This should not be the only time spent with the disciple, but it should be the main teaching and training time other than while spending time with them when teachable moments occur.

This is a planned time together for prayer, fellowship, accountability, and a teaching or training time. The discipleship meeting can be during a meal, in the afternoon, morning, night, or any time that both parties can commit to meeting together. I've found that early in the morning one day per week on the same day has been the most effective. Early in the morning there is less likely a potential postponement or change in the meeting time or place. Also, most people will not have added pressure to get home, so that the time can be focused. Have the time whenever it is convenient for both parties involved.

Teaching and training involve a unique system, as well. Whether it is spending time alone with God each day (quiet time) in prayer and Bible study, or evangelism, it is important for the discipler to do the act in front of the disciple.

Next, show them how.

Then, do it with them.

Let them do it with your assistance, then let them do it without your help. As the old saying goes, you can catch fish and feed someone once, or you can take them with you and teach them to fish and feed them for a lifetime. The goal is that they can confidently do it all without you. We are trying to build in them competence in every area of discipleship so that they can reproduce themselves.

After they have a clear conviction about the area, and you have given them the tools and training necessary to be competent, the next step is consistency. In my experience, consistency usually is only probable when there is pre-set accountability of the person's desired areas on a regular basis. This needs to be a part of the weekly discipleship group meeting. Maybe there is a verse each week that the group is committing to memory, a bad habit they are trying to give up, or a positive habit they are trying to build.

These are the areas for which people need accountability. Also give them items that will hold you accountable. This will be a mutually challenging and encouraging time each week for everyone involved.

CHAPTER 6

IN WHICH AREAS DO I NEED TO TRAIN THE DISCIPLE?

These areas are not clearly defined in *The Bible*, but one can conclude many principles, perspectives, and applications from the Word of God. Included on the next page is the list of the areas that have worked for me in the process of discipleship. On the next page is a detailed list of the areas in which a believer needs to be grounded. They are truly the basics of Christianity.

These basics are the focus of the rest of this book.

I have read many books that have radically changed my life on the subject of discipleship, however, none of them gave me the specific areas in which to teach and train the disciple. One of the motivations of this book is to present a list and the detailed information about each topic so that it could be all-inclusive, both for the discipleship leader and the disciple.

These areas cover three main establishing goals found on page 23:

- our relationship with God
- our relationship with ourselves
- and our relationship with others

Under each heading you will find the list of areas to invest into a disciple. The next page is also a chart to determine the growth of your disciple with 'The Three Questions" and "The Three Cs" implemented with the areas.

You may have noticed the areas on the Discipling Map that expressed the training for the Moldable Disciple. The discipler needs to train the Moldable Disciple in the areas of their relationship with God, their relationship with self, and their relationship with others. Many other areas develop later in the disciple's development, such as character, knowledge, skills, and vision. As you see the marks represented by growth in their life you will be able to assess their needs.

The following page is simply another tool to utilize however you see fit. You may need to alter it to meet the needs of your ministry or culture. Remember that all of this information is a tool it is not meant to replace the Word of God, nor the working of the Holy Spirit in a person's life.

Establishing and Equipping Disciples

1) Where do you want to take them?

_____

1) Where are they now?

_____

3) What is the next step?

_____

	Conviction	Competence	Consistency
A. Belief—			
1. Word of God	___	___	___
2. The Gospel	___	___	___
3. Grace	___	___	___
4. Lordship	___	___	___
5. Assurance	___	___	___
6. Position in Christ	___	___	___
7. Faith	___	___	___
B. Disciplines—			
1. Prayer	___	___	___
2. Bible Study	___	___	___
3. Church	___	___	___
4. Fellowship	___	___	___
5. Evangelism	___	___	___
6. Discipleship	___	___	___
7. Life Management	___	___	___
C. Leadership —			
1. TALENTS	___	___	___
2. Values	___	___	___
3. Vision	___	___	___
4. Goal Achieving	___	___	___
5. World Vision	___	___	___
6. Life Mission	___	___	___
7. TEAM	___	___	___

Each culture presents its own challenges, so adapt the information to meet those needs. You may be in an area in which you need to teach about the differences of Christianity and the area's other competing religions as a larger focus than the areas I have included.

My hope is that you develop your own establishing list to meet the needs of your specific target people group. These areas are simply the ones that have worked in my life and in those I have discipled.

There are clear areas that utilize "The Three Questions" and "The Three Cs." The blanks left next to each category can be used to check off the area as you have covered it in the life of the disciple. This will enable you to help chart their growth through the conviction, competence, and consistency portion of the chart.

The design of "The Three Questions" is to keep the discipler focused on the vision of moving their disciple continually to the next level in each area in their life. Remember that Jesus clearly had His men with Him for other teachable moments. Those are the moments that are not planned, nor expected. However, these are the moments that can bring about the most impact in the life of the disciple. Be aware of teachable opportunities that will arise as you spend time with your disciples.

CHAPTER 7

WHY ISN'T EVERYONE A DISCIPLER?

> *"Everyone who is to come after me, must deny himself, take up his cross daily and follow me."*
> *Luke 9:23*

We must remember that if this process of discipleship were easy, everyone would already be doing it. I relate discipleship to the chin-up or pull-up exercise. I managed a World Gym for a while. During January, when all the new members would be hogging all the machines, I would hear the complaining of the long-term members who were committed to working out regularly. I would simply tell them that there is never a line for the pull-up bar. It is one of the most difficult exercises, and yet it delivers some incredible results. It is truly much like discipleship. The work is hard, long, and has lasting results. But the results are not immediate.

Why isn't everyone who claims to be a Christian a discipler?

Although it seems easy on paper, it is not. There are many demands on a discipler that allow Satan to mislead a multiplying Christian and make him believe that he is not getting anywhere with his disciples. The rewards of discipleship are very slow and difficult to see. The discipler's time is no longer all his own. There is a lack of public recognition in discipleship. Few will see you laboring.

> *"There is no public recognition—just a deep, personal sense of satisfaction and fulfillment in seeing lives changed right before your eyes."*
> *Allen Hadidian*

Although your idea of discipleship may have been crushed by the last two paragraphs, there is a great reward for being obedient to what God has called every believer to do.

As so eloquently written by Walter A. Henrichsen in his book, *Disciples Are Made Not Born* (Henrichsen, 1988), he states:

> *"Discipleship is our opportunity to tap into the infinite resources of*

God. It is our chance to give our lives to
significance rather than mediocrity. . .
However, Jesus also warns us to
weigh the cost and weigh it well, for
discipleship will cost us something. It will
cost us our lives. But the results are
infinitely greater than the cost, so
much greater that one would be
foolish to turn down such an offer."

Summarized in a quote by Jim Elliott, the famous missionary to tribal Indians in Ecuador,

"He is no fool who gives up
what he can't keep to gain that which
he cannot lose."

He must know that more than most as he lost his life trying to reach the Auca Indians with the Gospel of our Lord Jesus Christ.

Bill Hull stated clearly in an article, "The Greatest Test of Faith," published in *The Discipleship Journal* 1983, Issue 13, (Hull, 1983)

"A reproducing Christian is the
most awesome weapon in our Father's
arsenal, and if there is any way Satan
can divert this Christian's attention or

sap his energy, he will endeavor to do it."

Bill Hull continues by saying,

> *"Many laymen and women are only spectators in the spiritual conflict because there are not many pastors or Christian leaders who are committed to disciplemaking. . . This is a sad but true commentary on the Bride of Christ, and it will not change until Christian leaders are willing to sacrifice fame and quick church growth in order to get serious about the job description Christ gave us. . . Determine what God's top priority is for your group, and then do it. Don't be led astray by any other calling. . . You have your marching orders. . . To summarize, disciple making takes courage, time and patience, and flexibility—and therefore, great faith."*

I remind you of the last words of our Lord and Savior Jesus Christ before He ascended into Heaven to sit at the right hand of the throne of God.

"All authority in Heaven has been given to me. Therefore, go and make disciples of all nations, baptizing them in the name of the Father and of the Son and the Holy Spirit, and teaching them to obey all that I have commanded you. And surely I will be with you to the very end of the age."
Matthew 28 18-20

This verse is often referred to as the great commission. I believe that is exactly what Jesus is doing in this verse. He is commissioning the people present to do that very thing...

"go and make disciples of all nations."

He didn't say go and make church members. He didn't say go and make deacons or elders. He said go and make disciples of all nations. There are many who believe that the "go" means to be a foreign missionary, and others who say it is as you go. I am not sure which is true, however, I do know that we need both. The 'where' may be up for discussion, but the 'what' is very clear;

"make disciples of all nations."

Very clearly it states to baptize them in the name of the Triune God. I do believe that this is a water baptism, and I'm going to keep the main thing the main thing. Whether it is submersion or sprinkle or a believers' baptism or a sign of the covenant relationship with God, I am going to leave that up to you. The importance is that we baptize them in the name of the Father, the Son, and the Holy Spirit.

Often called the great omission of the great commission:

"and teaching them to obey all that I have commanded you."

Obviously, this is a huge portion of the discipleship process. Too many churches count converts and baptisms as success. That is success, however, it is just the beginning. Discipleship must become an accepted part of the local church for the fruit to remain.

"And surely I will be with you to the very end of the age,"

What a promise for all those who are committed and commissioned by Jesus himself to the process of discipleship. He gives us the clarity that He is there working in us and through us to grow us and the disciple up in the Lord. He is with us to the very end of the age. He can and will do His part, and He has commissioned us to do our part.

GO AND MAKE DISCIPLES!!
GO AND MAKE DISCIPLES!!
GO AND MAKE DISCIPLES!!

It is the Christians mandate, our job, our responsibility, a necessity for all believers to hear our commission, the great commission. <u>Go and make disciples!!</u>

CHAPTER 8

THE WORD OF GOD

"The Bible contains the mind of God, the state of man, the way of salvation, the doom of sinners, and the happiness of believers. Its doctrines are holy, its precepts are binding, its histories are true, and its decisions are immutable.

Read it to be wise, believe it to be safe, and practice it to be holy. It contains light to direct you, food to support you, and comfort to cheer you. It is the traveler's map, the pilgrim's staff, the pilot's compass, the soldier's sword, and the Christian's charter.

Here paradise is restored, heaven opened and the gates of Hell disclosed. Christ is its grand subject, our good its design, and the glory of God its end. It should fill the memory, rule the heart, and guide the feet.

Read it slowly, frequently, prayerfully. It is a mine of wealth, a paradise of glory, and a river of pleasure. It is given to you in life, will be opened at the judgment, and be remembered forever. It involves the highest responsibility, rewards the greatest labor, and condemns all who trifle with its holy contents."

Author Unknown

There are many tests used to determine whether a document is true. They are almost never completely conclusive because of the number of original documents usually is so small, and the length of time those number of documentations have existed is so extensive.

However, when it comes to *The Bible*, the Word of God, those normal struggles for conclusive determination are nonexistent. C. Sanders writes about these tests in his book, *Introduction to Research in English Literary History* (Sanders, 1952).

Therefore, we are going to look at his three tests to discover that *The Bible* is exactly what it claims to be—The Word of God. The three tests we are going to look at are bibliographical, internal, and external.

THE BIBLIOGRAPHICAL TEST

> *"The Bibliographical Evidence Test is the examination of textural transmission by which documents reach us. In other words, not having the original documents, how reliable are the copies we have with regard to the number of manuscripts and the time interval between the original and extant copy?"*
>
> C. Sanders (Sanders, 1952)

The larger the number of manuscripts of a certain document the better it allows one to research the validity of the text. The book with the second largest number of manuscripts is *The Iliad* (Homer, 1844) with 643 original manuscripts. Of the 643 manuscripts there were approximately 40,000 contradictions. It was believed to have been written in 900 B.C.

The latest manuscripts of *The Iliad* were dated to 400 B.C. Obviously, the longer the period of time the manuscripts date the easier for a larger number of contradictions. However, with these facts being as they are *The Iliad* is believed to be the true account of the what the author, Homer, constructed.

There have been more manuscripts of *The Bible* found than any other book. *The Bible* has more than 24,000 original manuscripts. Of those 24,000 original manuscripts of *The Bible* that have been found, 21,000 of them were identical. Three thousand of the manuscripts had contradictions that affected a grand total of seven verses and four words.

However, even these minor contradictions did not change the meaning of a single verse. The earliest copy of *The Bible* is determined to date back to 125 A.D. Due to this Bibliographical Test, we can conclude that *The Bible* is the truest book in existence today.

THE INTERNAL EVIDENCE TEST

The Internal Evidence Test determines if the written record is credible and to what extent. Sanders states, "In this test one must listen to the claims of the documents under analysis and not assume fraud or error unless the author disqualifies himself by contradictions or known factual inaccuracies.

In *The Bible,* no contradictions have been proven and many alleged contradictions have been cleared by archaeology and systematic understanding. The document under analysis is studied to see if it disqualifies itself through self-contradiction. *The Bible* says a lot about itself. We are only going to look at a few of the facts *The Bible* says about itself—its preservation and its production.

    The Bible has a great claim of preservation.

> *"For you have been born again,
> not of perishable seed, but of
> imperishable, through the living and
> enduring word of God. For, all men
> are like grass, and all their glory is like
> the flowers of the field; the grass
> withers and the flowers fall, but he
> word of the Lord stands forever."*
>   *I Peter 1:23-25*

Jordan and Justin Drake eloquently described in *The Evidence Bible* by Ray Comfort (Comfort, 2011)

> *"No other book has been so
> attacked throughout history as The
> Bible. In A.D. 300, the Roman*

*emperor Diocletian ordered every
Bible burned because he thought that
by destroying the Scriptures he could
destroy Christianity. Anyone caught
with a Bible would be executed. But
just 25 years later, the Roman
emperor Constantine ordered that 50
perfect copies of the Bible be made at
government expense. The French
philosopher Voltaire, a skeptic who
destroyed the faith of many people,
boasted that within 100 years of his
death, The Bible would disappear
from the face of the earth. Voltaire
died in 1728, but The Bible lives on.
The irony of history is that 50 years
after his death, it is believed that the
Geneva Bible Society moved into his
former house and used his printing
presses to print thousands of Bibles."*

The Bible is great in its production. The writing of *The Bible* is said to be all inspired by God breathing the words into the life of the person writing the book.

*"All scripture is God-breathed
and is useful for teaching, rebuking,
correcting and training in
righteousness."*
    II Timothy 3:16

The Bible was written by more than 40 authors of many different occupations. They wrote in three different languages on three different continents over a period of 1,500 years. When these 66 books were joined together, they fit in perfect harmony without contradiction.

Yet, *The Bible* has one great theme and central figure—Jesus Christ. All of this would be impossible unless *The Bible* had one supreme Author– and it did—The Holy Spirit of God.

*"And we have the word of the
prophets made more certain, and you
will do well to pay attention to it, as to
a light shining in a dark place, until the
day dawns and the morning star rises
in your hearts. Above all, you must
understand that no prophecy of
Scripture came about by the prophet's
own interpretation. For prophecy
never had its origin in the will of man,*

but men spoke from God as they were
carried by the Holy Spirit."
II Peter 1:19-21

THE EXTERNAL EVIDENCE TEST

The External Evidence Test is the third Sanders test. It is used to determine if other historical documents or truth findings contradict what the document itself conveys. In other words, are there facts outside itself that disprove facts claimed within itself?

> *"It may be stated categorically that no archaeological discovery has ever controverted a biblical reference."*
> *The renowned Jewish archaeologist, Nelson Glueck from More than a Carpenter, Josh McDowell (McDowell, 1986)*

In Isaiah 44:28-54:1, he states that King Cyrus, who wasn't alive yet, would rebuild the temple at the city of Tyre. This writing came 100 years before the birth of Cyrus, and 100 years before the destruction of the Temple.

Ezekiel made seven prophecies about Tyre. One of Ezekiel's prophecies was that King Nebuchadnezzar would tear down the city of Tyre. Ezekiel made this prophecy in 592 B.C., which was approximately 20 years before King Nebuchadnezzar tore down the city in 573 B.C. Alexander the Great came in 332 B.C. and laid the city flatter. Yet, the exact person Isaiah said would rebuild the temple in Tyre, did just that.

There are countless examples of the prophetic nature of Scripture that lead to only one answer—it is truly the God-breathed, Holy Spirit-inspired Word of God. It touches the subjects of heaven and Hell, salvation and damnation, eternity past to eternity future, as well as the day-to-day activities of life no matter where you live or in what time period you live.

"If you were to take the sum total of all authoritative articles ever written by the most qualified of psychologists and psychiatrists on the subject of mental hygiene—if you were to combine them and refine them and cleave out the excess verbiage—if you were to take the whole of the meat

*and none of the parsley, and if you
were to have these unadulterated bits
of pure scientific knowledge concisely
expressed by the most capable of
living poets, you would have an
awkward and incomplete summation
of the Sermon on the Mount. And it
would suffer immeasurably through
comparison. . . Here. . . Rests the
blueprint for successful human life
with optimism, mental health, and
contentment."*

*T. J. Fisher and L.S. Hawley
from A Few Buttons Missing about
Jesus' morality as expressed in the
Sermon on the Mount (Fisher, 2017)*

In conclusion, these tests are used to prove that non-Christian and Christian books are written by whom they are stated to be written by and to classify if they are a reliable source of those writings. Based on these tests, *The Bible* has passed the tests with the highest score of any book ever. We can confidently believe that the Bible is the Word of God just as it claims.

> *"All scripture is God-breathed
> and is useful for teaching, rebuking,
> correcting and training in
> righteousness, so that the man of God
> may be thoroughly equipped for every
> good work."*
> *II Timothy 3:16-17*

THE BIBLE IS GOD-BREATHED AND USEFUL

> *"All Scripture is God-breathed
> and is useful for teaching, rebuking,
> correcting and training in
> righteousness."*
> *II Timothy 3:16*

This verse describes several ways the Scripture is useful for us today. The first area that the apostle Paul mentions *The Bibles'* use is with what this verse is teaching. *The Bible* gives very clear instruction in the right things we should be doing. From the statement above by T.J. Fisher the Sermon that Jesus preached gave the best instruction for "mental hygiene." It was basically the "blueprint for successful human life."

63

The Bible is full of right ways to live to protect us and to fulfill an abundant life for us.

> *"The thief comes to steal, kill, and destroy; but I came that you might have life and life more abundantly."*
> *John 10:10*

The Bible is very clear on rebuking, as well. Rebuking is the process of telling us when we are living out of the protective boundaries of God's ways. Rebuking is basically telling us when we are wrong.

The Bible also takes some more steps for telling us when we are wrong, and also for correcting us by telling us how to get right. By correcting us, *The Bible* is not just a list of dos and donts, it is a guide to help us live a successful, fulfilled life. God is committed to us in that He accepts us as we are, but He loves us enough to know that our extreme happiness is determined by a change in us.

He doesn't just want us to know when we are right or wrong, He also wants to give us guidance on how to be right. The next step in the verse is that *The Bible* trains us. The training comes by repetition of going to the Word of God for guidance and learning the truths of Scripture. Through that repetition we are trained in the right ways to do things the next time, therefore removing the rebuking and correcting stages of *The Bible's* use.

> *"We have much to say about all this, but it is hard to explain because you are slow to learn. In fact, though by this time you ought to be teachers, you need someone to teach you the elementary truths of God's word all over again. You need milk, not solid food! Anyone who lives on milk, still being an infant, is not acquainted with the teaching about righteousness. But solid food is for the mature, who by constant use have trained themselves to distinguish good from evil."*
> *Hebrews 5:11-14*

Notice in this section of God's Word He is explaining some of the process of spiritual growth through the knowledge and understanding of Scripture. He points out that we are all at different levels in our growth and many need someone to point out the elementary truths again. The mature have trained themselves through constant use. The repetition is essential. We must understand thoroughly the Word of God to know Him and to follow Him.

HOW CAN WE UNDERSTAND WHAT *THE BIBLE* SAYS?

There are several ways to grow in your understanding of the Word of God. They are to hear it, read it, study it, memorize it, and meditate on its applications to your life. It exists for guidance, strength, comfort, and to lead us to the loving arms of its author.

HEAR THE WORD OF GOD

Hearing is the easiest way to get the Word of God in you, consequently, for most Christians it is the only way they use. One can simply attend a church and hear the Word of God. One can hear the Word of God on a television or radio program. There are many audio ministries that will allow you to listen to the Word of God in your car while driving down the road.

"Consequently, faith comes from hearing the message, and the message is heard through the word of Christ." Romans 10:17

Therefore, we must hear the Word of Christ to grow in our faith and personal relationship with Him.

READ THE WORD OF GOD

However, hearing is just one of the ways we can get the Word of God into us. The next step is by reading it.

We have come a long way since the Christians of earlier generations. There were times when it was illegal to have the Holy Scriptures. There were other times when it was reserved for only certain people to read *The Bible*. Today, it is the best-selling book in the world every year. You can find a Bible just about anywhere.

"When your words came, I ate them; they were my joy and my heart's delight, for I bear your name, O Lord God Almighty."
Jeremiah 15:16

Jeremiah's view was that reading and knowing God's Word was his joy and delight.

"Day after day, from the first day to the last, Ezra read from the Book of the Law."

Nehemiah 18:18

> *"They stood where they were
> and read from the book of the Law of
> the Lord their God for a quarter of the
> day, and spent another quarter in
> confession and in worshiping the Lord
> their God."*
> *Nehemiah 19:3*

We must also read the Word of the Lord, *The Holy Bible.*

STUDY THE WORD OF GOD

If we only hear and read *The Bible,* we may still struggle to understand the depths of its applications to our lives. This next step of studying *The Bible* is the area that most Christians struggle the most. Studying is hard work. To understand any of the depths of an omniscient, omnipotent, and omnipresent God will take work.

Bible study is not simply reading or hearing, it is taking the time to sit down with your Bible, prayer, pen, and paper and really diving into the significance of the information.

> *"It has been said that The Bible is shallow enough for the youngest baby to swim in with never any fear of drowning, yet at the same time deep enough that the greatest of theologians can dive into and never be able to touch the bottom."*
>
> *Howard Hendricks, Living By the Book (Hendricks, 2007)*

I promise that if you study the Scriptures deep enough you will still never be able to understand completely the mind of God. Yet, He will reveal great and unsearchable things that you do not already know.

> *"For my thoughts are not your thoughts, neither are your ways my ways, declares the Lord. As the heavens are above the earth, so are my ways higher than your ways and my thoughts above your thoughts.*
>
> *Isaiah 55:8-9*

He will radically change your prospective on life through the power of His Word and the guidance of the Holy Spirit. However, the specifics on how to study *The Bible* will continue in Chapter 8 and involve having a daily quiet time.

MEMORIZE THE WORD OF GOD

Another way to get *The Bible* into our life is to memorize it.

> *"How can a young man keep his way pure? By living according to your word. I seek you with all my heart; do not let me stray from your commands. I have hidden your Word in my heart that I might not sin against you."*
>
> *Psalm 119:9-11*

By memorizing the verses in *The Bible* we arm ourselves with the truth, so that when questionable decisions or circumstances arrive we are prepared to make the right choices. There are a lot of other benefits to memorizing God's Word. It is very useful when people challenge our faith about God and *The Bible* to have the verses memorized that back up our beliefs.

Also, it is of great encouragement when we struggle, to be able to claim the promises of God because we have them memorized. *The Bible* is full of people who memorized Scripture. Many of the New Testament believers would quote Scripture in the defense of their faith. We need that option just as much, if not more, than they dd. We need to memorize God's Word.

Spend some time reading in the book of Psalms, Chapter 119 to see more clearly the view these people had on the importance of knowing the Word of God. They attributed the Word of God as their very life blood. Just about every verse in that chapter directs us back to the reasons for hiding God's Word in our heart.

MEDITATE ON THE WORD OF GOD

The last step in getting God's Word in us that can radically change our direction and choices in life is to meditate on His word. To truly utilize *The Bible* as our guide and charter we must take every step we can to ensure the working of God's Word in our lives to strengthen us, guide us, comfort us, and lead us in the right path.

By meditation, I am not referring to sitting in the floor with your legs crossed, candles lit, and chanting aloud. I am referring to thinking deeply in an attitude and awareness of prayer, while trusting God to reveal truths to us that we need to apply to our life.

"Do not let this book of the Law depart from your mouth; meditate on it day and night, so that you may be careful to do everything written in it. Then you will be prosperous and successful. Have I not commanded you? Be strong and courageous. Do not be terrified; do not be discouraged, for the Lord your God will be with you wherever you go."
Joshua 1:8-9

"Blessed is the man who does not walk in the counsel of the wicked or stand in the way of sinners or sit in the seat of mockers. But his delight is in the law of the Lord, and on his law he meditates day and night. He is like a tree planted by streams of water, which yields its fruit in season and whose leaf does not wither. Whatever he does prospers."
Psalm 1:1-3

There are several ways to get the Word of God in you. With the results mentioned in the previous verses, we need to take all five steps as often as possible. We need to know, understand, and apply the Scripture to our lives so that we can follow the plan God has for us.

> "God has written a grand narrative for each of us and is committed to keeping us from writing a lesser narrative than the one He has already written."
> Bob Buford, In his book, Game Plan (Buford, 1998)

> "For we are God's workmanship created in Christ Jesus to do good works that He prepared in advance for us to do."
> Ephesians 4:10

We can hear, read, study, memorize, and meditate on the significance of the word of God. However, we must not simply do this to gain more understanding; rather we must go to the Word of God to know (conocer) the author.

> "And we know that the Son of God has come and has given us

*understanding, **so that we may know
him** who is true; and we are in him
who is true, in his son Jesus Christ.
He is the true God and eternal life."*
I John 5:20

MORE VERSES FOR FURTHER STUDY AND REFLECTION

Psalm 1:1-3
I Peter 2:2
Hebrews 4:12
James 1:22
Matthew 4:4
John 8:31
Psalm 119:10

CHAPTER 9

THE GOSPEL— THE LIFE, DEATH, BURIAL, AND RESURRECTION

*"Now I would remind you, brothers, of the gospel I preached to you, which you received, in which you stand, **2** and by which you are being saved, if you hold fast to the word I preached to you—unless you believed in vain. For I delivered to you as of first importance what I also received: that Christ died for our sins in accordance with the Scriptures, that he was buried, that he was raised on the third day in accordance with the Scriptures, and that he appeared to Cephas, then to the twelve."*
I Corinthians 15:1-5

The Gospel can be the most freeing or the most enslaving thing for the believer. The believer who understands the Gospel lives in light of it, worships because of it, relates with all humanity in the results of it, believes in it, trusts through it, stands with the strength from it, relies on it, cares because of it, and dies in comfort because of it.

The Gospel is everything to the believer who understands it.

> *"The marker of those who understand the gospel of Jesus Christ is that, when they stumble and fall, when they screw up, they run to God and not from him, because they clearly understand that their acceptance before God is not predicated upon their behavior but on the righteous life of Jesus Christ and his sacrificial death."*
> *Matt Chandler, The Explicit Gospel, p.211 (Chandler)*

For the believers who do not understand the Gospel, it can enslave them. They will try to accept God's love by their work instead of his. They will attempt to please God with all their future actions, while continuing to doubt themselves and their stance before God. Instead of trusting in the finished work of God through Jesus Christ's life, death, burial, and resurrection they will continue to trust in their own work in life and death. The strain of walking around on eggshells and believing that each time they step out of line that God is going to punish them will result in a joyless Christianity that looks more like worship of themselves and their ability to be moral, rather than worshipping the one who has endured the punishment in their place—Jesus.

Most believers live their entire life not truly understanding the Gospel and what God has done for them in the precious gift of His Son.

WHAT IS THE GOSPEL?

The Gospel is the life, death, burial, and resurrection of Jesus Christ. We should all be clear on that. For some, this would be the entire chapter. Yes, just this one statement. They would be correct on a test. However, without understanding the implications of the Gospel of Jesus Christ to our hearts and life, we completely miss the true meaning of the Gospel.

Jesus was born of a virgin, Mary, in the little town of Bethlehem. He was constantly under attack because of the predictions about the savior being born in that region. He was the son of Joseph, a carpenter.

Jesus worked with his father. This is a hard-working profession. At an early age, Jesus and his parents were going through town, and they lost him.

After searching for a while, they found him with the teachers of the Law. He was speaking in such a way about the Law that everyone was amazed. Jesus continued to grow in favor and stature with man.

When he was 30 years old, he began his public ministry at his own baptism, where he was baptized by his cousin, John the Baptist. At his baptism, the Holy Spirit descended from heaven like a dove upon him, and God spoke of him by saying, "This is my son, in whom I am well pleased."

Jesus chose 12 disciples to follow him. They walked with him, talked with him, ate with him, ministered alongside him. He trained them to train others. Jesus performed many miracles that lead to many people becoming followers of him and of the things that he taught.

So many people were following him that the leaders of his time grew jealous and worried that an uprising could occur. To stop any kind of rebellion against their teaching and way of life they had him killed.

In 33 years of life, Jesus never sinned. He was 100% God and 100% Man—the God Man. Although he was God, he humbled himself to be made in human likeness, to become a servant, and to live the example that God requires of all his followers.

In the life that Jesus lived, he set the perfect example of the way that God requires of all of us. We all fall short in comparison to Jesus' life. The Bible calls this missing the mark of perfection—sin.

"For all have sinned and fallen short of the Glory of God."
Romans 3:23

The Bible is very clear that the wages of sin is death. Therefore, because we were unable to live the life that God required of us, we are all due his wrath toward sin. This death is an eternal separation from God in Hell.

"For the wages of sin is death, but the gift of God is eternal life, through Christ Jesus our Lord."
Romans 6:23

In the illustration on Page 42, we have Sinful man on the left mountaintop, and Holy God on the right. Man constantly tries to get across to God through his good actions. None of the attempts of sinful man to get across to God are good enough. He falls short every time.

A wage is what you get for what you do. That which we have done is sin—missed perfection. The result or payment for this is death—eternal separation from God in Hell.

A gift is something given solely because of the love of the giver. A gift is not earned or repaid. The gift of God is eternal life. This gift of eternal life comes only through the life, death, burial, and resurrection of Jesus. He lived the life we couldn't live and then died as the sacrificial substitution for us. He not only took our sin and debt of sin upon himself as he died in our place, but he passed his perfect record of righteousness to us. In this, God sees the perfection of Jesus in place of our sin.

> *"God made him, who knew no sin, to be sin for us, so that in him we might become the righteousness of God."*
> *II Corinthians 5:21*

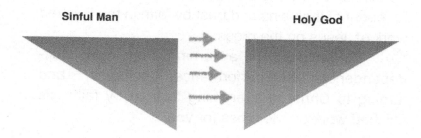

Sinful Man   **Holy God**

Romans 6:23 *"For the wages of sin is death, but the gift of God is eternal life through Christ Jesus our Lord.*

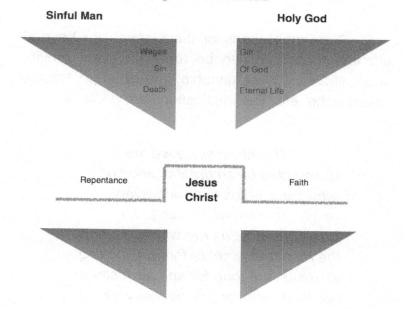

Sinful Man   **Holy God**

Wages   Gift
Sin   Of God
Death   Eternal Life

Repentance   **Jesus Christ**   Faith

81

The response of Holy God to sinful man is to give the precious gift of Jesus Christ. To live the perfect life and die the sinner's death in our place is to repent of their sins and trust by faith in the finished work of Jesus on the cross.

Repentance is a turning from your self-dependence, self-performance, self-guilt, and turning to Christ in everything to trust by faith His finished work on the cross for you.

WHAT ARE THE IMPLICATIONS OF THE GOSPEL?

The implications of the Gospel are beyond our imagination. It can be found in every movie, show, life activity, relationship, goal, triumph, failure, catastrophe, etc. The implications are endless.

"Therefore since we are surrounded by so great a cloud of witnesses, let us lay aside every weight, and sin which clings so closely, and let us run with endurance the race that is set before us, looking to Jesus, the founder and perfecter of our faith, who for the joy that was set before him endured the cross,

despising the shame, and is seated at
the right hand of the throne of God."
Hebrews 12:1-3

Many people understand the basics of the Gospel for belief in Jesus for salvation, but too many miss the practical implications to their personal lives after salvation. The implications of The Gospel are great in the life of the believer who understands them. The Gospel implications can be seen in all relationships, work, and worship.

The implications of The Gospel to relationships allow those relationships to build up one another instead of constantly comparing ourselves and competing with one another. We can see that we are all on equal ground—sinners saved by The Gospel. In all relationships as we consider how much Christ forgave us, it encourages us and enables us to forgive. Several relationships that are affected by The Gospel are family, leadership, and authority-based relationships.

In marriages, understanding The Gospel is the first thing I teach prospective spouses. If they can learn to forgive often and quickly, then they are set up to be successful in their relating with each other for their lifetime. This type of forgiveness is only possible when people understand that they already get what they don't deserve in The Gospel.

Understanding The Gospel gives an attitude of gratitude rather than a feeling of entitlement. Once we quit focusing on our own pride, arrogance, and self-exultation, we are then free to focus on our spouse instead of ourselves. The Gospel brings freedom to love without expectation.

For siblings, The Gospel allows for less comparison and competing for attention, because the Gospel demands that attention and praise be placed on the one who paid the price for us—Jesus. The Gospel also allows great forgiveness to flow throughout the sibling relationships as we look to Jesus to finish what He has begun. He enables us to forgive.

In relationships that deal with authority, we often are resistant to be humble. We can come to these relationships with great pride, which can be misplaced frustration. Maybe those in authority do not lead the way we desire, or maybe they are not Christians. God has placed all governing authority over us on purpose and for a purpose. He hasn't "fallen asleep at the wheel" in these relationships. He is still committed to being the "founder and perfecter of our faith" in these relationships also.

Maybe it is that we feel that we don't have to submit to a leader because they don't believe the way that we do, or perhaps they are not a strong leader. We must realize that God has a plan to perfect us in some areas in that as well. Ultimately, we must trust God in the midst of all situations.

> *"Consider it pure joy, my brothers whenever you face trials of many kinds, because you know that the testing of your faith produces perseverance, and perseverance must finish its work so that we may be complete not lacking anything."*
> *James 1:1-2*

Without The Gospel, we see that what we deserve is Hell.

The Gospel has great implications with our effort or work. Too often we have bought into an idea that God loves us based on our performance rather than on His own perfect performance in Christ Jesus. If we do not understand The Gospel, then our work will always be in hopes that God will love us more because we worked harder or sacrificed greater. However, this is a great misbelief.

> *"...but God shows his love for us in that while we were still sinners, Christ died for us."*
> *Romans 5:8*

We must understand that our right standing before God is not generated by our work, rather it is in the person and work of Jesus Christ alone. We do not work in order to be forgiven We work because we already are forgiven. We do not work in order to get Jesus or his love. We work because we already have Him and his love. Therefore, we are not loved because of what we do. We are loved because of what HE HAS DONE!

> *"The universe shudders in horror that we have this infinitely valuable, infinitely deep, infinitely rich, infinitely wise, infinitely loving God, and instead of pursuing him with steadfast passion and enthralled fury — instead of loving him with all our heart, soul, mind, and strength; instead of attributing to him glory and honor and praise and power and wisdom and strength — we just try to take his toys and run. It is still idolatry to want God for his benefits but not for himself."*
>
> *Matt Chandler, The Explicit Gospel, p.39–40 (Chandler)*

If we truly understand The Gospel, it will lead us into the true worship of Jesus. We no longer have to look at ourselves in the mirror to perfect ourselves. That is God's job. We are to look to Him as the "founder and perfecter of our faith." Once we realize that he has paid all the debt that we owed God, that he has absorbed all the wrath that God had in store for us, we are indeed free to worship Him in spirit and in truth.

THE GREATEST NEED FOR EVERYONE IS THE GOSPEL

The greatest need for the person who is a not-yet believer is The Gospel. The greatest need for the person who is a believer is The Gospel—not the disciplines, not more meetings with the church, not more peers who love Jesus—but more JESUS.

On the timeline below there are three points of our life represented: Birth, Spiritual Birth and Death. There are two time periods represented the time from Birth to Spiritual Birth and the time from Spiritual Birth to Death. The person who has been born, but not yet born again through Spiritual Birth has a great need of the Gospel, so that they can trust in Christ for salvation. However, the greatest need of the person who has trusted Christ for Salvation is also the Gospel.

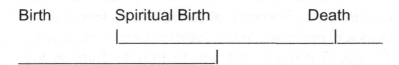

Birth   Spiritual Birth   Death

Too often we try to pour into the life of the new believer all the things that they need to get busy doing, while leaving off the continued education on the implications of The Gospel.

The amazingly freeing thing about this truth is that we now know what everyone on the planet needs to hear from us—The Gospel. It is not simply those without Christ who need to hear The Gospel, but those in Christ, as well.

We all need the constant reminder of how we got to where we are, and to remember that the only thing that differentiates us from the not-yet believer is The Gospel. This not only humbles us, but it also engages us to want to share how God has changed us.

HOW CAN WE REMAIN GOSPEL CENTERED?

The main issue we face daily is a continued lack of the ability to stay focused on The Gospel in every area of our lives. Too often, we allow ourselves to focus on ourselves, our circumstances, our weaknesses, or even our strengths. All of these focuses create the idea that we are the focus, rather than focusing on Christ.

"Therefore, since we are surrounded by so great a cloud of witnesses, let us also lay aside every weight, and sin which clings so closely, and let us run with endurance the race that is set before us, 2 looking to Jesus, the founder and perfecter of our faith, who for the joy that was set before him endured the cross, despising the shame, and is seated at the right hand of the throne of God. 3 Consider him who endured from sinners such hostility against himself, so that you may not grow weary or fainthearted"
Hebrews 12:1-3

To counter the idea of focusing on ourselves, we must look to Jesus. In some versions of the Bible, this verse literally says to fix our eyes on Jesus. We must preach the gospel to ourselves everyday as a constant reminder of the person and work of Jesus Christ on our behalf. This act of pressing into Christ and his substitutionary sacrifice on the cross for us will bring great relief and freedom in our walk with the Lord.

> *". . . it is intimated, that he burned with so much fervor for God's glory that he was possessed by such a desire to promote his kingdom, that he forgot himself, and was, as it were, absorbed with this one thought, and that he so devoted himself to the Lord that he was grieved in his soul whenever he perceived His Holy Name exposed to the slandering of the ungodly."*
>
> *John Calvin (Calvin, 2009), in his commentary on Romans does a great job describing how David, the psalmist, was able to fix his eyes on God. (Calvin's Commentary on Romans Volume 19)*

The greatest challenge to understand The Gospel of Our Lord and Savior Jesus Christ is to realize that he took our sin upon himself and suffered the penalty of it, while taking his perfect record and passing it on to us along with the reward of it.

"For our sake, God made him who knew no sin, to be sin for us, so that in Him we might become the righteousness of God."
II Corinthians 5:21

MORE VERSES FOR STUDY AND REFLECTION

I Corinthians 15:1-5
Romans 5:8
II Corinthians 5:21
Ephesians 2:8-9
Galatians 2:20-21
Romans 6:23
Romans 3:21-23

CHAPTER 10

GRACE—GOD'S UNMERITED FAVOR TO THOSE WHO DESERVE HIS WRATH

COMMON GRACE VS. SPECIFIC GRACE

Common grace is the existence of God's goodness to all people to allow things such as their life, breath, abilities to eat, organs to function, limbs to operate, mind to think, ears to hear, eyes to see, heart to pump blood, emotions, etc. These common graces are not equal to all, as all of us know some who were not blessed with all of these common graces. This does not take away from God's blessings to allow some of these graces.

Grace is undeserved favor. We did not do anything to deserve these gifts or abilities. Each one is a precious grace from God. We do not think of these graces very often. We take them for granted until we meet those who do not have them, and then we are humbled by the fact that we get them. Yet even then we often do not praise God for his goodness to grant these common graces to us as we did nothing to earn them.

Specific Grace is what the rest of this chapter is about.

Specific Grace is the additional blessing of God to people who again did not deserve, work for, nor earn His blessing. This blessing of specific grace is to those who He has revealed Himself to in a personal relationship through faith in the life, death, burial, and resurrection of Jesus Christ. This Specific Grace is what we call salvation.

Salvation comes when God pursues us with His love and calls us into a personal relationship with Him. He then grants us repentance and faith to trust Him for eternal salvation. This salvation can only occur because Jesus lived the perfect life that we were incapable of living, and then he died the death we deserved in our place.

He became the substitutionary sacrifice for us. He took our sin upon himself and gave us his righteousness.

> *"For our sake he made him to be sin who knew no sin, so that in him we might become the righteousness of God."*
>
> *II Corinthians 5:21*

The entirety of Scripture is a picture of God's Grace, either in its prophetic message of the coming cross of Jesus Christ, its proclamation of the Christ who has come, or in its endless comparisons to the depth of the results of Christ's cross.

ADAM AND EVE

A picture of God's goodness, faithfulness, and joy in having a relationship with man. When they failed Him, instead of killing them as He had said they would surely die, He kicked them out of the Garden. However, He clothed them with skin of other animals to provide some protection.

This is a picture of God's grace. He chose not to end their lives even though they deserved it. He also took another of his creation's life to provide a covering for their body—a picture of the future grace He would provide by killing the perfect one of all his creation to provide a covering of the sins of all who would believe.

DAVID AND GOLIATH

A picture of God's provision of One who would win the battle and the result would be victory for all in the battle. This is not a picture for us to be like David. We are part of those shaking in our armor, unable to defeat the giant. God provided One who would defeat all the giants of our life for us and pass the victory on to us. David is a representation of the future Jesus who would ultimately take on the greatest battle and win over life and death to give us the victory in both.

JONAH AND THE BIG FISH

A picture of God's commitment to have His name proclaimed, and the clear comparisons to the ONE who would come to proclaim and be proclaimed. Jonah was in a cold dark place for three days, ultimately spit out in a place where people didn't want to hear about the relief and deliverance by God for them. Jesus was placed in a cold dark tomb, but on the third day arose and preached relief and deliverance to those for whom He died.

Every story occurred, and every one points us to the Christ who would take upon himself the wrath of God in our place. His sinless life which allowed him to die a sinner's death in our place has truly been described in all of Scripture, all of creation, and is now readily available for us to understand and proclaim.

WHY IS GRACE NEEDED?

"What then? Are we Jews any better off? No, not at all. For we have already charged that all, both Jews and Greeks, are under sin, 10 as it is written:

> *"None is righteous, no, not one;11 no one understands; no one seeks for God.*
> *12 All have turned aside; together they have become worthless; no one does good, not even one."13 "Their throat is an open grave; they use their tongues to deceive." "The venom of asps is under their lips." 14 "Their mouth is full of curses and bitterness."*
> *15 "Their feet are swift to shed blood; 16 in their paths are ruin and misery, 17 and the way of peace they have not known." 18 "There is no fear of God before their eyes." 19 Now we know that whatever the law says it speaks to those who are under the law, so that every mouth may be*

stopped, and the whole world may be held accountable to God. 20 For by works of the law no human being will be justified in his sight, since through the law comes knowledge of sin."
                              Romans 3:9-19

Grace is needed, because just as we see God's goodness, graciousness, and blessing in The Old Testament as well as in The New Testament, we also see God's wrath in the Old and New Testaments. God's wrath goes out to the sin of all the world.

His judgment of sin is righteous. His penalty for sin is legitimate. His anger toward sin is undeniable. The difference in the Old Testament and The New Testament in God's wrath is that we see Him destroy cities, harden hearts, bring death and destruction to armies in The Old Testament and The New Testament reads like a love story.

This love story is due to his Grace. His wrath is demonstrated throughout The New Testament, as well. We miss it because we are no longer the object of His wrath—His Son is.

All of the wrath of God was absorbed by Jesus, in our place. The New Testament does read like a love story because of the love of the Father to allow his only begotten son to endure the wrath we deserved based on His indescribable love for us.

> *"But now the righteousness of God has been manifested apart from the law, although the Law and the Prophets bear witness to it— 22 the righteousness of God through faith in Jesus Christ for all who believe. For there is no distinction: 23 for all have sinned and fall short of the glory of God, 24 and are justified by his grace as a gift, through the redemption that is in Christ Jesus, 25 whom God put forward as a propitiation by his blood, to be received by faith. This was to show God's righteousness, because in his divine forbearance he had passed over former sins. 26 It was to show his righteousness at the present time, so that he might be just and the justifier of the one who has faith in Jesus."*
> *Romans 3:21-26*

If we don't understand the depravity of our own hearts, then we do not understand the fierceness of the rebellion against God.

> *"The Lord saw that the wickedness of man was great in the earth, and that every intention of the thoughts of his heart was only evil continually. 6 And the Lord regretted that he had made man on the earth, and it grieved him to his heart. 7 So the Lord said, "I will blot out man whom I have created from the face of the land, man and animals and creeping things and birds of the heavens, for I am sorry that I have made them."*
> *Genesis 6:5-7*

To understand the sin against God, we must recognize that the sin is not only the act—the motive—but also to whom the offense was against that must be measured. If I were to slap my brother in the face, it would result in a fight. If I were to slap a policeman in the face, it would result in him placing me in handcuffs. If I were to slap the President in the face, it could result in an onslaught of bullets from the Secret Service agents who protect him.

You see, the act intensifies based on whom it is targeted against. We have committed countless sins against the Almighty King of Kings. We should end up in Hell. Yet, by his mercy, He doesn't give us what we deserve—Hell. And by His Grace, He gives us what we don't deserve—Heaven. To really understand Grace, we must realize that as horrible as our rebellion against God is to Him, he deems its deserved penalty is Hell.

> *"For the wages of sin is death,… but thankfully the verse continues with, "… but the gift of God is eternal life through Christ Jesus our Lord."*
> *Romans 6:23a*

As we better understand the seriousness of our sin and the penalty therein, we can better understand the price that has been paid by His only begotten son for God to purchase us as sons and daughters.

God did not just cancel the debt of our sin. Rather, He satisfied it with His son's death so that he could adopt us as righteous sons and daughters. He did not simply say its ok, go on your way. Instead, He welcomed us into his family.

> *"For by grace you have been saved through faith. And this is not your own doing; it is the gift of God, 9 not a result of works, so that no one may boast."*
> *Ephesians 2:8-9*

To fully understand His Grace, we must understand that we bring nothing but our sin to the equation—not our good works plus Jesus. Jesus brings his perfect, spotless record, and we bring our record of sin, high treason against the King of Kings, and the Lord of Lords.

Then, we trade places. Yes, literally, Jesus takes our sin record and the penalty that comes with it, and we take His righteous record and the benefits that come with it.

He receives our eternal death sentence, and we receive right standing with God and an eternal life as a reward. All of this is not of ourselves, it is the gift of God.

How amazing is this grace?

For many of us this may be the first time we really understand the depth of this hymn by John Newton, published in 1779 (Newton, 1779):

"Amazing grace! How sweet the sound
That saved a wretch like me!
I once was lost, but now am found;
Was blind, but now I see.
'Twas grace that taught my heart to fear,
And grace my fears relieved;
How precious did that grace appear
The hour I first believed.
Through many dangers, toils and snares,
I have already come;
Tis grace hath brought me safe thus far,
And grace will lead me home.
The Lord has promised good to me,
His Word my hope secures;
He will my Shield and Portion be,
As long as life endures.
Yea, when this flesh and heart shall fail,
And mortal life shall cease,
I shall possess, within the veil,
A life of joy and peace.
The earth shall soon dissolve like snow,
The sun forbear to shine;
But God, who called me here below,
Will be forever mine.

When we've been there ten thousand years,
Bright shining as the sun,
We've no less days to sing God's praise
Than when we'd first begun."

MORE VERSES FOR STUDY AND REFLECTION

James 4:6
Ephesians 1:7
Acts 15:11
Romans 1:15-17
Romans 5:20-21
Romans 6:14
Romans 11:6

CHAPTER 11

LORDSHIP OF JESUS CHRIST

CAN JESUS BE YOUR SAVIOR AND NOT YOUR LORD?

According to *The Bible,* Jesus is the Savior, and He is the Lord of Lords. He is the ruler of all of creation. He is the LORD.

Can Jesus be your Savior and not your Lord?

Only if the Jesus that you worship and claim to be your Savior is not the Jesus of *The Bible*. If the Jesus of *The Bible* with whom you have placed your faith for salvation, then He must also be Lord of your life.

Jesus is the Savior who was prophesied about in The Old Testament, who came down from heaven to be born of a virgin, lived the perfect life we cannot live, and died a brutal death in our place to save us from the sin penalty of eternal death. We all agree that we need a Savior. He has been proclaimed with great detail.

105

"Who has believed what he has heard from us? And to whom has the arm of the Lord been revealed? For he grew up before him like a young plant, and like a root out of dry ground; He had no form or majesty that we should look at him, and no beauty that we should desire him.

He was despised and rejected by men; a man of sorrows, and acquainted with grief; and as one from whom men hide their faces he was despised, and we esteemed him not.

Surely he has borne our griefs and carried our sorrows; yet we esteemed him stricken, smitten by God, and afflicted.

But he was pierced for our transgressions; he was crushed for our iniquities; upon him was the chastisement that brought us peace, and with his wounds we are healed.

All we like sheep have gone astray; we have turned—every one—to his own way; and the Lord has laid on him the iniquity of us all.

*He was oppressed, and he was
afflicted, yet he opened not his mouth;
like a lamb that is led to the slaughter,
and like a sheep that before its
shearers is silent, so he opened not
his mouth.*

*By oppression and judgment
he was taken away; and as for his
generation, who considered that he
was cut off out of the land of the
living, stricken for the transgression of
my people?*

*And they made his grave with
the wicked and with a rich man in his
death, although he had done no
violence, and there was no deceit in
his mouth.*

*Yet it was the will of the Lord to
crush him; he has put him to grief;
when his soul makes an offering for
guilt, he shall see his offspring; he
shall prolong his days; the will of the
Lord shall prosper in his hand.*

*Out of the anguish of his soul
he shall see and be satisfied; by his
knowledge shall the righteous one,
my servant, make many to be*

accounted righteous, and he shall
bear their iniquities.
    Therefore I will divide him a
portion with the many, and he shall
divide the spoil with the strong,
because he poured out his soul to
death and was numbered with the
transgressors; yet he bore the sin of
many, and makes intercession for the
transgressors.
    Isaiah 53

While we all agree that we need a Savior, we may not understand the implications of having Jesus as our Savior and Lord.

Most of us do not truly understand what Lord means. This is also a point of contention when discussing the reign and the rule of Jesus Christ. We like to read *The Bible* as a book of God bless me, God love me, God provide for me, God take care of my enemies, God save me, etc.

What we do not like is when *The Bible* actually states that Jesus is the Lord over our lives instead of us being the Lord of our own life. "It's my life and I can live it however I see fit," is our arrogant statement of control.

However, control is a myth. Not one of us has control of even our own tongue, much less where we would be born, to whom, our socioeconomic or racial background, class system, physical or mental ability, personality, giftedness, first language, or even our natural hair color or lack thereof. We are not in control.

For many, this is scary. To finally begin to understand that at any moment a truck could spin out of control down our own street and run through our breakfast room and kill us, or that lightning could strike us dead as we sit and read this right now. We are not in control, but we know One who is.

I choose to trust Him absolutely. After learning about Him and growing to know Him personally through His word and His Spirit, I want Him in control of every detail of my life. He has displayed himself to be gracious to all, even through the common graces, and even moreso by His specific grace he has revealed to those He has adopted as His own family.

I would not want a Savior who was not Lord. Too many struggle to give up the control of their lives because of the thought that we know what is best for ourselves. Historically, this could not be further from the truth. Biblically this could not be further from the truth. If you go back and read your own journals this could not be further from the truth. We do not make good Lords of our lives. Especially when we have one who is all knowing, all powerful, and everywhere at the same time. His ways are not our ways. His thoughts are not our thoughts, He is far superior in his wisdom.

"He is the image of the invisible God, the firstborn of all creation. For by him all things were created, in heaven and on earth, visible and invisible, whether thrones or dominions or rulers or authorities—all things were created through him and for him. And he is before all things, and in him all things hold together. And he is the head of the body, the church. He is the beginning, the firstborn from the dead, that in everything he might be preeminent. For in him all the fullness of God was pleased to dwell, and through him to reconcile to himself all things, whether on earth or in heaven, making peace by the blood of his cross. "…in everything he might be preeminent."
Colossians 1:15-20

Preeminent is defined as -eminent above or before others; superior; surpassing: Synonyms: distinguished, peerless, supreme. See dominant. (Dictionary.com)

The word Lord appears in *The Bible* more than 7,800 times. The leading Greek and Hebrew words for Lord are "despot" and "kurios." The meanings of the word Lord in *The Bible* from these root words in its original language are most closely translated as; despot—Lord, Master, and Absolute Ruler; curios—to exercise Lordship over, controller, supreme in authority, to rule. (Strong's Exhaustive Concordance)This is obvious that Jesus being Lord makes Him the controller, absolute ruler, supreme in authority, master of everything in existence.

HE IS LORD. IS HE YOUR LORD?

"Have this mind among yourselves, which is yours in Christ Jesus, who, though he was in the form of God, did not count equality with God a thing to be grasped, but emptied himself, by taking the form of a servant, being born in the likeness of men. And being found in human form, he humbled himself by

becoming obedient to the point of
death, even death on a cross.
Therefore God has highly exalted him
and bestowed on him the name that is
above every name, so that at the
name of Jesus every knee should
bow, in heaven and on earth and
under the earth, and every tongue
confess that Jesus Christ is Lord, to
the glory of God the Father."
Philippians 2:5-11

He is Lord of all and every knee shall bow and every tongue shall confess that Jesus Christ is Lord in Heaven and on earth and under the earth. That verse includes everyone who believes and everyone who does not believe will still bow and confess that Jesus Christ is Lord. Whether we acknowledge that this side of death doesn't change that HE IS LORD!

WHAT DOES IT LOOK LIKE FOR US TO ACKNOWLEDGE HIM AS LORD?

For this explanation of us acknowledging Jesus Christ as Lord, I am going to use an analogy. This analogy is only meant to take it as far as I do. If our life is the business, Jesus is the owner, and we are the manager. Jesus is Lord, and we are manager. As the manager, we should do that which meets the requirements and requests of the owner.

We managers must act and run the business as if the owner was present at all times and according to His wishes. This is the practical application of Lordship. We are the managers of this life He has given us, and we must lead as a response to His will for our life. We lead our lives as a response to the goodness and graciousness of God to allow us to have this life, and we lead it for His Glory and pleasure.

On a lifetime basis this management seems impossible. On a day-to-day basis we can follow His lead in a step-by-step basis. He has freed us from all condemnation in Christ Jesus.

> *"Therefore, there is now no condemnation for those in Christ Jesus. . ." Romans 8:1*

He has paid the price for our sin through His Son's death, burial, and resurrection.

> *"...You are not your own, for you were bought with a price. So glorify God in your body."*
> *I Corinthians 6:19-20*

He has given us everything we need to follow Him.

> *"His divine power has granted to us all things that pertain to life and godliness,…"*
> *II Peter 1:3*

He has adopted us into his family.

> *"…but you have received the Spirit of adoption as sons, by whom we cry, "Abba! Father!"*
> *Romans 8:15*

He has given us His love letter to guide our steps.

> *"Your word is a lamp to my feet and a light to my path."*
> *Psalm 119:105*

He has even planned out in advance that which He requires we should do.

> *"For we are his workmanship, created in Christ Jesus for good works, which God prepared beforehand, that we should walk in them."*
> *Ephesians 2:10*

So, if he has done all of this how do we live this Lordship in our lives?

> *"And he said to all, "If anyone would come after me, let him deny himself and take up his cross daily and follow me."*
> *Luke 9:23*

There is a real bowing of our heads in humility to our own desires and feelings to be able to deny ourselves. This step, while being the first step, is the easiest of the three mentioned in Luke 9:23.

This idea of finally admitting that my record of doing things my way has not always worked out for my good and for the good of those around me. For most of us, it has worked out to be a steamy pile of dung. When we can finally be honest with ourselves, we can consciously admit that we have failed miserably and that we are all jacked up.

These recognitions should lead us to a foregone conclusion that the answer is to deny ourselves. To turn from our ways and acknowledge the ONE who should be the Lord of our lives. This act of doing this is what *The Bible* calls repentance. Repentance is a gift from God. It is the ability to admit where we have missed the mark of perfection and turn from those ways to HIM for forgiveness and leadership.

The second step in this process is the act of taking up our cross daily. The context still remains with the idea of dying to yourself, yet also lends itself to the recognition that the cross meant for us was taken through a substitutionary sacrifice of Jesus Christ in our place. So, to take up our cross daily can imply the realization of remembrance of the price Christ Jesus paid for us in His death, for our sake.

> *"For our sake he made him to be sin who knew no sin, so that in him we might become the righteousness of God."*
> *II Corinthians 5:21*

This recognition daily allows us to walk with Jesus in the reflection of Jesus' sacrifice for us. We realize that he died the death we deserve although he lived the life we should live. The understanding of the cross in this way empowers us with the overwhelming desire to please God.

The third step in the process is to follow Christ. Too often in Christendom we have this "easy believism" that we believe permits us to have Jesus as our Savior, yet it allows us to follow Him when it is convenient for us. We are often lacking in recognizing the price that was paid for us and therefore, we do not consider the cost to follow Jesus in the details of life.

To follow Jesus is to live as He lived, to walk as he walked, to teach as he taught, to train as he trained, to serve as he served, to finish the work God gave us to do as He finished the work God gave him to do. He gave us the example of how to live, and he also empowers us to live.

What it means to practice the Lordship of Jesus Christ is to ask ourselves in any and every situation what the Lord of all the earth would desire from us in that situation. We respond as faithful managers of the days he has given us, and with the gifts he has given us for His Glory.

MORE VERSES FOR FURTHER STUDY AND REFLECTION

Matthew 7:21-23
I Corinthians 6:19-20
II Corinthians 5:15
John 5:30
Romans 12:1-2
Psalm 37:3-5
Luke 9:23

CHAPTER 12

ASSURANCE

"And this is the testimony, that God gave us eternal life, and this life is in his Son. Whoever has the Son has life; whoever does not have the Son of God does not have life. I write these things to you who believe in the name of the Son of God that you may know that you have eternal life."
I John 5:11-13

Many believers struggle with understanding the Gospel because they lack assurance of their salvation. Too often we are taught to act right, be better, and live a better life. Recently, someone who knew me before I was a Christian said to a friend of mine, "Man he was wild, but he has gotten his life together now."

This type of statement that we can easily state nonchalantly about a person having been changed by the Grace of God through the Gospel of Jesus Christ just cheapens The Gospel. We cannot just get our life together. The requirement is perfection.

There is no possible way for us to attain perfection because of our sin nature and desires. Because of that sin nature and desire within each of us we are enticed by sin.

> *"But each person is tempted when he is lured and enticed by his own desire. Then desire when it has conceived gives birth to sin, and sin when it is fully grown brings forth death."*
> *James 1:14-15*

All of us have failed with this requirement.

> *"for all have sinned and fall short of the Glory of God."*
> *Romans 3:23*

Because of this failure to live according to the righteous requirements of the law, God provided himself to come down as the man Jesus Christ, live the perfect life that we could not live, then pay the debt of our sin by dying on the cross for our sins. Jesus not only paid the debt of our record of unrighteousness, but He gave us His record of righteousness. We literally stand before God perfect in Christ.

We often struggle to believe The Gospel and its present and eternal implications. Eternally we have a spotless record before God. We are promised eternal life, and we can know for sure that we have this because of Christ alone. However, we soon forget that this record has been resolved the moment we accept Christ as our Lord and Savior.

We lose sight of The Gospel and run to self-help, fixing our life, or getting our life together all on our own. We say things like, "God helps those who help themselves." What? Not a single verse in *The Bible* says or even implies that to be true. He works in us in spite of us, and not because of us.

The truth is that the Christ of the Cross solves the issue of eternity, and then he also solves the issues of today. We have been sold a lie that Jesus saves us, then we work really hard to please God. The truth is that Jesus saves us, therefore, we please God.

When we focus on bettering our lives, we set ourselves up to one of two evils: either absolute failure, or self-exaltation. Only when we can rest in the finished work of Christ Jesus can we focus on Him as we have been instructed.

". . .fix your eyes on Jesus the
author and finisher of our faith…"
Hebrews 12:2

We are only free to worship someone other than ourselves once we understand our salvation has come to us by grace through faith in the finished work of Jesus Christ.

"For by grace you have been
saved through faith. And this is not
your own doing; it is the gift of
God, not a result of works, so that no
one may boast."
Ephesians 2:8-9

When we focus on our behavior modification to please God, we run the risk of never being able to please Him. The other side of the argument is that when we work diligently and by some depravity of understanding in our own minds, we believe we have changed ourselves into a person that pleases God by what we do—we exalt ourselves, which is idol worship. We are only free, when we realize that Jesus sets us free, not our obedience.

> *"He saved us, not because of works done by us in righteousness, but according to his own mercy, by the washing of regeneration and renewal of the Holy Spirit, whom he poured out on us richly through Jesus Christ our Savior, so that being justified by his grace we might become heirs according to the hope of eternal life."*
> *Titus 3:5-7*

God's word is filled with promises that we can claim about Him, His work, and how He deals with us. He has promised us assurance of salvation, that "you may know that you have eternal life."

> *"Truly, truly, I say to you, whoever hears my word and believes him who sent me has eternal life. He does not come into judgment, but has passed from death to life."*
> *John 5:24*

> *"For with the heart one believes and is justified, and with the mouth one confesses and is saved. For the Scripture says, "Everyone who believes in him will not be put to shame." For there is no distinction between Jew and Greek; for the same Lord is Lord of all, bestowing his riches on all who call on him. For "everyone who calls on the name of the Lord will be saved."*
> *Romans 10:10-13*

We can have assurance of our salvation based on the person and work of Jesus Christ alone as described in God's word. He also assures us of forgiveness in a way that most of us do not think through enough.

> *"If we confess our sins, he is faithful and just to forgive us our sins and to cleanse us from all unrighteousness."*
> *I John 1:9*

> *"as far as the east is from the west, so far does he remove our transgressions from us."*   *Psalm 103:12*

> *"For I will be merciful toward their iniquities, and I will remember their sins no more."*
> *Hebrews 8:12*

He forgives us, cleanses us, removes our sins infinitely away from us, and remembers them no more. It is truly amazing forgiveness. He pardons our sin and does not place us on parole. His forgiveness is not contingent on our behavior, instead it is according to his loving kindness toward us.

WHAT CAN TAKE AWAY YOUR SALVATION?

> *"For I am sure that neither death nor life, nor angels nor rulers, nor things present nor things to come, nor powers, 39 nor height nor depth, nor anything else in all creation, will*

be able to separate us from the love
of God in Christ Jesus our Lord."
Romans 8:38-39

What cannot take away the love of God in Christ Jesus?

Death - you can't lose it when you die.

Life - you can't lose it while you are alive.

Angels - can't take it from you.

Demons - can't steal it from you.

Present - you can't do anything right now to lose it.

Future - you can't do anything in the future to lose it.

Powers - the devil can't cause you to lose it, nor can any other authorities.

Height - nothing above you can remove it from you.

Depth - nothing below you can keep it from you.

Nor Anything else in all creation - can separate us from Christ.

We are assured through God's word that once He has saved us there is nothing that can separate us from His love for us in Christ Jesus our Lord. This truth that He loves us this well should warm our hearts. His promise is even deeper than this. He has promised us that nothing can take away his love for us, and He has secured that all who come to Him will be kept by Him for eternity.

> *"And this is the will of him who sent me, that I should lose nothing of all that he has given me, but raise it up on the last day. For this is the will of my Father, that everyone who looks on the Son and believes in him should have eternal life, and I will raise him up on the last day."*
> *John 6:39-40*

This verse conveys Jesus speaking of the will of God the Father for Him and us. He not only keeps us, but will raise us up with Him on the last day.

WE CANNOT COME TO CHRIST UNLESS HE DRAWS US

> *"No one can come to me unless the Father who sent me draws him. And I will raise him up on the last day."*
> *John 6:44*

If we do not have the ability to come to Christ, then we do not have the ability to leave him. If your salvation is not something that you found, how can it be something that you can lose. Jesus later clarifies this in verse 65 of Chapter 6 of John when he said,

> *"This is why I told you that no one can come to me unless it is granted him by the Father."*

We don't even have the ability to be saved without the desire and drawing from God the Father.

The drawing in this verse is also a bit misleading. We think that he seduces us into believing and trusting in him. This drawing is better translated as dragging. I came to believe in Christ kicking and screaming, because I enjoyed being the Lord of my life.

I didn't dislike God, I just did not want to give up control of my life. He later used a fraternity brother of mine, Clay Duncan, to share the truth of the Gospel with me. After about three months of studying *The Bible* with Clay, God began working in my heart to reveal the truth about who He is and what He had done for me through the person and work of Christ on the cross.

On January 30, 1992 God dragged me to His throne as Lord of Lords and King of Kings. I bowed at his feet and confessed that Jesus Christ is Lord. He granted me the faith to trust in Him and gave me the gift of repentance to turn from my sin unto Him for forgiveness.

Having paid a huge ransom for me, God then adopted me as His son. He removed my sin from me and placed it on Jesus, and then he took Jesus' record of perfection and placed it as my record before Him. Therefore, I can say that I am Saved! I am Saved! For forever and always Jesus Saved ME!

We can all be assured of our salvation because it is not left in our hands to earn, repay or maintain. Jesus did everything required to save us and sustain us for eternity. The full price for us has been paid. This chapter has been saturated with the word of God. We can take God at his word.

> *"God is not man, that he should lie, or a son of man, that he should change his mind. Has he said, and will he not do it? Or has he spoken, and will he not fulfill it?"*
> *Numbers 23:19*

MORE VERSES FOR FURTHER STUDY AND REFLECTION

John 10:28
Philippians 1:6
I Corinthians 5:17
Romans 8:16
Hebrews 10:22
Hebrews 12:1-2
II Timothy 1:12

CHAPTER 13

POSITION IN CHRIST

In Christianity, many people clearly understand the teachings on salvation and how they can be sure of their eternal destiny through Jesus Christ's death, burial, and resurrection. However, very few begin to comprehend the implications of that truth to our position before God.

We just take the eternal life in Heaven as the blessing that comes from salvation, therefore, missing the clear blessing of Christ in this life. To further understand these implications we must look into the depths of who we once were and compare this with who God says that we are now.

WHO WERE WE?

We were created to enjoy God's presence in a perfect place called the Garden of Eden. He cared for us. He provided for us. He spent time with us. He brought us together with a mate, and He placed us in authority of the rest of his creation. And, He truly loved us. He did, however, give us one rule, and we disobediently committed high treason against the King of Kings and the Lord of Lords.

"The Lord saw that the wickedness of man was great in the earth, and that every intention of the thoughts of his heart was only evil continually. And the Lord regretted that he had made man on the earth, and it grieved him to his heart. So the Lord said, "I will blot out man whom I have created from the face of the land,…"
Genesis 6:5-7

"And you, who once were alienated and hostile in mind, doing evil deeds,…"
Colossians 1:21

"For we ourselves were once foolish, disobedient, led astray, slaves to various passions and pleasures, passing our days in malice and envy, hated by others and hating one another."
Titus 3:3

We were slaves to sin. Through our desires and actions, we literally displayed the bondage to its control over our lives. We were separated from God, alienated from Him, hostile to Him in our minds, and grew in wickedness. We were by nature objects of wrath, and we allowed our own hearts to be idol factories by what we desired in passions and pleasures.

WHO ARE WE NOW?

> *"he has now reconciled in his body of flesh by his death, in order to present you holy and blameless and above reproach before him,..."*
> *Colossians 1:22*

God was patient with our sin nature, and sent his son to reconcile us to himself through Christ's death, burial, and resurrection. He paid the debt of our sin in this act of substitutionary sacrifice, and He presents us holy and blameless before God. He removes the sin and the stain. There is no more sign of the sin left on us. Jesus paid for it all to be removed from us completely and placed upon Him.

He has made us a **New Creation**.

"Therefore, if anyone is in Christ, he is a new creation. The old has passed away; behold, the new has come."

I Corinthians 5:17

Our record of wrong was placed on Jesus and therefore removed completely from us. Everything from our old self has passed away. We have been made new.

There is now **No Condemnation.**

"There is therefore now no condemnation for those who are in Christ Jesus. For the law of the Spirit of life has set you free in Christ Jesus from the law of sin and death. For God has done what the law, weakened by the flesh, could not do. By sending his own Son in the likeness of sinful flesh and for sin, he condemned sin in the flesh, in order that the righteous requirement of the law might be fulfilled in us, who walk

not according to the flesh but
according to the Spirit."
Romans 8:1-4

He has brought out the verdict of "no condemnation" on that man / "no condemnation" on that woman. The condemnation that was due us also was placed on Jesus. There is no condemnation leftover from that which was paid for by Jesus. God doesn't condemn us, and if He doesn't, then no one else can.

God has also set us free from the law of sin and death. We will taste sin and death, but it no longer has a sting. The payment has been paid. We are free because Jesus paid the debt of our sin, and He fulfilled the righteous requirements of the law and passed his record of perfection to us.

We have become **Children of God and Heirs**.

"But to all who did receive him,
who believed in his name, he gave
the right to become children of God,"
John 1:12

"For all who are led by the Spirit of God are sons of God. For you did not receive the spirit of slavery to fall back into fear, but you have received the Spirit of adoption as sons, by whom we cry, "Abba! Father!" The Spirit himself bears witness with our spirit that we are children of God, and if children, then heirs—heirs of God and fellow heirs with Christ, provided we suffer with him in order that we may also be glorified with him.

Romans 8:14-17

"But when the fullness of time had come, God sent forth his Son, born of woman, born under the law, to redeem those who were under the law, so that we might receive adoption as sons. And because you are sons, God has sent the Spirit of his Son into our hearts, crying, "Abba! Father!" So you are no longer a slave, but a son, and if a son, then an heir through God."

Galatians 4:4-5

"But thanks be to God, that you who were once slaves of sin have become obedient from the heart to the standard of teaching to which you were committed, and, having been set free from sin, have become slaves of righteousness."
Romans 6:17-18

He replaced our record of wrong with His record of perfect righteousness, and He brought us into his family. Let that sit in for a minute. We understand forgiveness of people who do us wrong, but we do not turn around and adopt them as our children. This is altogether a larger step that God takes, and as a result shows His deep care for us. He is not just a judge who rules and reigns, judges, and executes. He is a Judge who is our Father.

I can't remember where I heard this story, or I would give credit to the author:

"A young woman was caught speeding. She later appeared in court and the judge asked her, "How do you plea?" She responded with, "guilty." He brought down the gavel and sentenced her to a fine, due immediately. Then the story changes a bit. The judge steps down from his place of high authority, walks over to the cashier, pulls out his wallet and pays the speeding fine for the young woman. The

judge was her father. He was a right judge, and he was a loving father. The fine had to be paid, and being a loving father, he paid the fine for her."

Like this Judge, God is righteous in his judgments, however He is also a loving father. He stepped down from his place of high authority and became the man Jesus Christ. Then he paid the fine of our sin by dying on the cross for us. He is a right judge and loving father.

No longer are we slaves to sin. Rather, we are sons and daughters of God. We are also heirs to all that is his.

We are Blessed with **Every Spiritual Blessing.**

"Blessed be the God and Father of our Lord Jesus Christ, who has blessed us in Christ with every spiritual blessing in the heavenly places, even as he chose us in him before the foundation of the world, that we should be holy and blameless before him. In love he predestined us for adoption as sons through Jesus Christ, according to the purpose of his will, to the praise of his glorious grace, with which he has blessed us in the

*Beloved. In him we have redemption
through his blood, the forgiveness of
our trespasses, according to the
riches of his grace, which he lavished
upon us, in all wisdom and insight
making known to us the mystery of his
will, according to his purpose, which
he set forth in Christ as a plan for the
fullness of time, to unite all things in
him, things in heaven and things on
earth."*

Ephesians 1:3-10

God has blessed us in Christ with every spiritual blessing. He chose us, made us holy and blameless before him, predestined us for adoption, redeemed us, and forgave us. He has truly done everything to change who we once were to make us who we are now in Christ.

We have a **Guaranteed Inheritance.**

*"In him we have obtained an
inheritance, having been predestined
according to the purpose of him who
works all things according to the
counsel of his will, so that we who
were the first to hope in Christ might*

*be to the praise of his glory. In him
you also, when you heard the word of
truth, the gospel of your salvation, and
believed in him, were sealed with the
promised Holy Spirit, who is the
guarantee of our inheritance until we
acquire possession of it, to the praise
of his glory."*
                    Ephesians 1:11-14

We have hope in Christ, and we have a guarantee of our inheritance through the promised Holy Spirit. This is not a "hope so," this is a "know so"—a guarantee. We are heirs, and we have a guaranteed inheritance from God.

As we understand our position in Christ we can be free to focus on Jesus in gratitude for what he has done to change us from sinners to saints, from orphans to adopted sons and daughters, from slaves of sin to slaves of righteousness, free from the law of sin and death, and with a guaranteed inheritance in Heaven.

Below is a love letter from God to us in relation to the new life he has given us:

To: You

From: God

Date: Today

RE: **What I think about you**

I want to tell you that I have known you since before the foundations of time. I even know the hairs on your head. I put you together on purpose and for a purpose. I looked at you and saw that you were fearfully and wonderfully made. I even created you in my image.

I also gave you gifts to prepare and equip yu for the plans I have for you. These gifts I've given are irrevocable. Don't neglect them. Exercise them and stir them up!

I want you to be confident about this: When I begin a good work in you I will carry it on to completion until the day of Christ Jesus.

Although you may encounter tribulations in this world, I want you to know that in me you have peace. Be of good cheer. I have overcome the world.

I am not slack concerning my promises. Forever my Word is settled in heaven and my faithfulness to all generations. When I have spoken it, I will also bring it to pass. When I have purposed it, I will also do it.

        You can look to me as a refuge and strength, a very present help in trouble. Cast your burdens upon me and I will sustain you. I shall never suffer the righteous to be moved. Come unto me when you labor and are heavy laden, and I will give you rest. For I am your rock, your fortress, your deliverer, your strength in whom you can trust. Though you fall you shall not be utterly cast down, for I will uphold you with my hand.

Don't listen to the ungodly, but rather delight yourself all day long in my Word. If you do, you will be like a tree planted by the river. You will bring forth fruit in season and whatever you do will prosper.

        Finally, I want you to know I love you. I love you so much I gave my only begotten Son. When you believe in Him, you will not die but have healing, freedom, victory, forgiveness and eternal life.

MORE VERSES FOR FURTHER STUDY AND REFLECTION

Genesis 1:27
I Peter 2:19
John 1:12
I John 3:1-2
Romans 8:14-17
Ephesians 1:3-5
II Corinthians 5:21

CHAPTER 14

FAITH

"Now faith is the assurance of things hoped for, the conviction of things not seen."
Hebrews 11:1

We have all heard the statements about faith that are often thrown around. For example, "I have faith in you. I have faith it will all work out. I have faith in this job. I have faith in this or that." The problem with these statements is that the strength of faith is not in how much trust we can muster, rather the strength of faith is found in the object of our faith. Too many people say that they have faith in a certain thing or person, when they are really trying to say, "I hope this job works out. I hope that this person doesn't disappoint me." Faith is assurance of things hoped for. There is no doubt in that faith, not because of the amount of faith, but because of what the faith is in. Faith is only as strong as the object of the faith.

In Christianity, our faith is placed in God—the Father, the Son, and the Holy Spirit. Therefore, we are trusting in the absolute creator and sustainer of all to work things out for our good and for His glory. We are also trusting in the finished work of Jesus Christ on the cross. Lastly, we are trusting by faith in the leading and empowering Holy Spirit, who resides in us. In Christianity, we do not have faith in objects. Instead, we have faith in a person—the three persons of God.

We often say that we only hope and trust in God. However, if we were truthful, we would say that we have faith in our ability to earn money, win friends, budget our money, provide for our family, protect our children, fix our car, and the list goes on. We may have the ability to do those things, but that does not ensure that these things will work out as we plan.

Everyone with children should have had the idea that it was their job to protect them. Many young children face horrifying deaths outside the control or protection of their parents. If you are reading this and have faced this, I am so sorry for your loss. Too many of us place faith in ourselves, rather than on God's ultimate plan for His glory and for our good.

WHAT IS FAITH?

According to **dictionary.com** faith is:

"confidence or trust in a person or thing"

Faith is trusting in, believing in, and having confidence in a person or thing. In Christianity, the person is God, and the thing is His Word. We do not have faith because we rely on Him and His word. We have faith, therefore, we rely on Him and His Word. The faith precedes the confidence, trust, and reliance.

The "assurance of things hoped for" and the "conviction of things not seen" come from us believing God at His Word. We hope, trust, rely, and believe God will do and has done what He says and has said He would do.

> *"God is not man, that he should lie, or a son of man, that he should change his mind. Has he said, and will he not do it? Or has he spoken, and will he not fulfill it?"*
> *Numbers 23:19*

The answer is yes, every time. The hard part is that He fulfills his promises in his perfect timing. Our timing is right now! We live in a "fast food, I want results now" culture. He does not always work the

145

way or at the pace that we want him to work. However, we can trust Him at His Word.

HOW DO WE GET FAITH?

Many people struggle with the idea that they have to muster enough faith to trust God with their lives—their provision, protection, future, areas of life they struggle with confidence, etc. The truth is that faith begins with God.

> *"looking to Jesus, the founder and perfecter of our faith, who for the joy that was set before him endured the cross, despising the shame, and is seated at the right hand of the throne of God."*
> *Hebrews 12:2*

He is the founder and perfecter of our faith. He begins it, and He finishes it. He works in both Saving Faith and Sustaining Faith. We will discuss this more as this chapter continues.

There are those who believe and teach that the reason that difficult situations have come your way is because you just don't have enough faith. Therefore, stating that if you just had enough faith then you would not have these circumstances in your life.

> *"Count it all joy, my brothers,*
> *when you meet trials of various kinds,*
> *for you know that the testing of your*
> *faith produces steadfastness. And let*
> *steadfastness have its full effect, that*
> *you may be perfect and complete,*
> *lacking in nothing."*
> *James 1:2-4*

Too quickly we discount the growth that God wants to do in our lives through trials, as times when we lack enough faith to miss these trials. Each trial has a purpose from God's point of view. Remember that He is the founder and perfecter of our faith. He knows exactly what to allow to come our way and how He can grow our faith through it to perfection.

SAVING FAITH AND SUSTAINING FAITH

Saving faith is the faith that God brings to us at the point that he changes our heart in such a way that He literally removes the hardened heart and replaces it with a soft heart that can know him.

*"I will give them a heart to
know that I am the Lord, and they
shall be my people and I will be their
God, for they shall return to me with
their whole heart."*
Jeremiah 26:7

*"And I will give you a new
heart, and a new spirit I will put within
you. And I will remove the heart of
stone from your flesh and give you a
heart of flesh."*
Ezekial 36:26

Through this heart transplant He births into us faith to trust Him as he puts a new spirit within us. Salvation occurs in us when by grace, God grants us faith to believe in Him.

*"For by grace you have been
saved through faith. And this is not
your own doing; it is the gift of God,
not a result of works, so that no one
may boast."*
Ephesians 2:8-9

God provides the faith to believe in Him. He initiates the change of heart. He extends his grace to us. He puts His Spirit in us. Saving faith has its beginning in God himself. He is truly the *"founder of our faith."*

Sustaining faith is the area that creates the most difference for many Christians. We do not often debate the act of God saving us by grace through faith, but when it comes to living the Christian life we tend to get a little fuzzy on some of the details. We want to claim credit. We want significance. We want to be the point of the story of our conversion and our growth. From a very young age we cry out, "Mommy look!"

We want to be recognized for our achievements. We desire to be praised. If sustaining faith is from God also, then He will be stepping on some of our toes of achievement.

> We are *"saved by grace through faith, not of our own doing, it is the gift of God, not a result of works, so that no one may boast"* Ephesians 2:8-9.

This verse is familiar to most Christians, but the implications of not boasting still raises its ugly head in our pride of walking with Jesus. "Oh, I read my Bible everyday." "I am at the church every time the doors are open." "I pray over every meal." etc. When are we going to surrender in this battle for pride of who does what in the changing of our lives? HE is the "founder and the perfecter of our faith. . . "

"I am sure of this, that He who began a good work in you will bring it to completion at the day of Jesus Christ."
Philippians 1:6

This faith that God begins, continues, and completes originates in Him. He gives it to us through the Holy Spirit who resides in us. This faith is for salvation and for sustaining us throughout the Christian life.

"Therefore, as you received Christ Jesus the Lord, so walk in him, rooted and built up in him and established in the faith, just as you were taught, abounding in thanksgiving. We walk not by faith not by sight.
Colossians 2:6-7

*"And without faith it is
impossible to please him, for whoever
would draw near to God must believe
that he exists and that he rewards
those who seek him. can we through
faith accomplish?*
        Hebrews 11:6

*"But whoever has doubts is
condemned if he eats, because the
eating is not from faith. For whatever
does not proceed from faith is sin."*
        Romans 14:23

*"If a man has faith in me, he
can do what I have been doing; he
can do even greater things than
these, because I am going to the
father. And I will do whatever you ask
in my name so that the son may bring
glory to the father. Ask me for
anything and I will do it."*
        John 14:12-14

Here we see Jesus saying even greater things than he had been doing. This was because he was going to the father and sending the counselor to us, to reside in us, and to empower us.

Through faith and for His glory, we can accomplish these things that he says we can accomplish, for his names' sake, not for our own. He even comes through with a promise to answer our prayers in the same way and for the same goal—to bring glory to the father. The real answer is anything that will bring God glory.

HOW DO WE LIVE A LIFE OF FAITH?

The real question now becomes how do we live out a life of faith?

> *"Therefore, since we are surrounded by such a great cloud of witnesses, let us throw off the sin that so easily entangles us, and let us run with perseverance the race marked out for us. Let us fix our eyes on Jesus, the author and finisher of our faith, who for the joy set before him, endured the cross, scorning its shame and sat down at the right hand of*

God. Let us consider him who
endured such opposition from sinful
men so that we will not grow weary or
lose heart."
Hebrews 12:1-3

The motivation to walk with God in faith comes from remembering the incredible cost He paid for us. He paid the cost to bring us into a relationship with Him through the life, death, burial, and resurrection of Jesus Christ. He has given us the gift of faith to save us and to sustain us. He has also given us faith to live the life he has called us to live.

"For we are Gods'
workmanship created in Christ Jesus
to do good works that he prepared in
advance that we should walk in."
Ephesians 2:10

MORE VERSES FOR STUDY AND REFLECTION

Hebrews 11:1   Galatians 2:20-21
Ephesians   Galatians 3:22
3:16-17   Romans 1:17
I John 5:11-13   Matthew 17:20

CHAPTER 15

PRAYER

When we talk about prayer, we often try to make it too haphazard of a thing so that we go about it flippantly, or we make it too complex a thing so that we must be at the perfect place in the perfect circumstances to pray correctly. We make prayer too complicated.

God has made the access to His throne too readily available to us for us to not go to Him in prayer often.

The Bible uses some powerful words to describe prayer: pray always, pray continually, pray in every situation, pray when you are anxious, pray when you are worried, pray when you are glad, pray when you are sad, pray for yourself, pray for others, pray for your enemies, pray for your leaders, pray for your followers, pray for your children, pray for your parents, pray for your culture; labor in prayer, work in prayer, cry out in prayer, request in prayer, ask in prayer, beseech in prayer, beg in prayer, etc. God has offered direct access to Him for all those who believe in Him.

WHAT IS PRAYER?

Prayer in its simplest definition is talking to God.

Prayer is not a methodological approach to getting God to do our bidding. It is not setting God up to be our fairy godmother or Santa Claus, who gives us whatever we ask. Prayer to us is a way of conversing with the Almighty God of the universe. Prayer to God is a way of displaying his sovereign faithfulness to us.

Sovereign faithfulness is God's way of answering our requests as long as they align with His sovereign plan for our lives, for our good and for His Glory. God knows the ripple effects of everything he does around the parameters of time.

Therefore, He knows how the answers to our prayers will affect our lives and those lives involved in our prayers long term. He cannot answer in a way that convolutes His sovereign will. We will speak more about this later in this chapter while addressing how to pray.

WHEN DO WE PRAY?

Jesus modeled prayer for us very well. He was in constant communication with His father. He prayed when he needed guidance. He prayed when things went well for him. He prayed when things went well for others. He prayed for God's wisdom and will while in solitude.

He prayed to God in his most trying moments. He prayed for others in their trying moments. He prayed all the time and every time he needed God's perspective and leading. He prayed while he walked, while he talked, when he ate, when he sat, when he preached, when he was beaten, and even while he was being crucified.

One of the most distinguishing characteristics of Jesus' life on earth was how often he communicated with his Heavenly Father.

Jesus also modeled the idea of prayer in solitude.

> *"And rising very early in the morning, while it was still dark, he departed and went out to a desolate place, and there he prayed."*
> *Mark 1:35*

We should also follow his lead and have a practice of praying in solitude on a regular basis. We can take prayer retreats to get our minds off of our own junk. We often spend our prayer time more focused on checking off a box on our to-do list just like taking out the trash than we do seeking God's face. We can take extended retreats in prayer for a day or half a day.

We can also take moment retreats in prayer for a half hour, or more. We need these times with God more than we realize until we actually take the time to meet with Him in this way. If we do not set aside the time, we generally will let go of the time it takes to retreat in prayer to some other item on our to-do list.

"Now as they went on their way, Jesus entered a village. And a woman named Martha welcomed him into her house. And she had a sister called Mary, who sat at the Lord's feet and listened to his teaching. But Martha was distracted with much serving. And she went up to him and said, "Lord, do you not care that my sister has left me to serve alone? Tell her then to help me." But the Lord answered her, "Martha, Martha, you are anxious and troubled about many things, but one thing is necessary. Mary has chosen the good portion,

which will not be taken away from
her." Luke 10:38-42

Too often, we are Martha when we need to be Mary.

We need to decide a time that we are going to pray. This discipline does not take away from the ongoing attitude of prayer throughout the day or the moments that we pray for God's provisions, or before important meetings, or simply driving down the road. We need the retreats from life's circumstances to just sit with God and pray. If we do not plan these retreats, they will not happen.

"If you fail to plan to pray, your
prayers will fall prey to other plans."
Author Unknown.

Set aside a time each month, week, day, and/or time of day to pray in solitude. During this time, utilize the section on How to Pray. Your prayer life will grow the more you do it. Maybe the first time you might spend 2-to-5 minutes, but eventually you will find yourself losing track of time in prayer.

REMEMBER—Prayer does not affect you more because of the minutes or hours that you spend in prayer. Rather, it affects you most as determined by the motive and heart behind the prayers.

HOW TO PRAY?

> *"If my people, who are called by my name, will humble themselves, seek my face, and turn from their wicked ways, then will I hear from heaven and forgive their sins and heal their land."*
> *II Chronicles 7:14*

Prayer is for those who God has brought into a personal relationship with himself through the substitutionary sacrifice of His only begotten son to adopt them as sons and daughters. Therefore, prayer is for those who are called by His name, Christians. He has allowed access to his throne of grace through undeserved favor. Prayer takes humility.

> *"Prayer honors God and dishonors self, it is man's plea of weakness, ignorance, want, a plea which heaven cannot disregard. God delights to have us pray."*

E.M. Bounds, Complete Works on Prayer (Bounds, 1990)

We must acknowledge our need for Him by humbling ourselves and coming to Him in that posture. In prayer, we must seek God's face, thus praying according to his name's sake and in accordance with his will. We must turn from our wicked ways for forgiveness of our sins, so that we pray in right standing with God.

> *"...then will I hear from heaven and forgive their sins and heal their land."*
> *II Chronicles 7:14*

> *"Whatever you ask in my name, this I will do, that the Father may be glorified in the Son. 14 If you ask me anything in my name, I will do it."*
> *John 14:13-14*

Asking for things and attaching "in Jesus' Name" to it is not a formula to getting whatever you want. The verse did not say that you can get whatever you want. "Whatever you ask in my name…", this means according to what will bring God's name Glory. For his name's sake, in his name, and for his glory are all interchangeable. He is saying in the book of John that those things that we request in accordance with His will and glory, that, He will do. This is not "I want a Farrari in Jesus' name."

How to pray in Jesus' name is to pray in sequence with His will, which is found in His word. To be an effective prayer warrior we need to know the Word of God. We need to know His Word so that we can pray it back to him. The greatest way to know if we are praying for His name's sake and for His Glory is to know His word. We can read what He wants in His word. Then we can pray for the things that He wants.

Another key area that will help your prayer life is to keep a prayer journal. This way of documenting prayers that you are trusting God to do for his Glory can be a constant reminder of His Sovereign Faithfulness. You can review your entire history of praying and see how and when God answers. You can do this through a simple prayer journal.

The Lord's prayer is an obvious place to go in scripture to see how to pray.

> *Pray then like this: "Our Father in heaven, hallowed be your name. Your kingdom come, your will be done, on earth as it is in heaven. Give us this day our daily bread, and forgive us our debts, as we also have forgiven our debtors. And lead us not into temptation, but deliver us from evil."*
>
> *Matthew 6:9-13*

There are four key parts to this prayer. They are adoration, confession, thanksgiving, and supplication. This method of prayer is an acronym called the ACTS pattern of prayer.

Adoration—The process of worshipping God for who he is—creator, sustainer, provider, etc.

Confession—The process of admitting wrong, that we have sinned, and pleading forgiveness.

Thanksgiving—The process of stating that for which we are thankful.

Supplication—The process of asking for needs of yourself and others.

WHY PRAY?

163

It is too easy for us to try and say that we pray so that God can go to work. We try to take too much credit. We claim that by praying we allow or give God permission to work. Can we even say that with a straight face? The almighty creator and sustainer of the universe is sitting around hoping that the created will request Him to do something. Prayer is designed to honor God.

Prayer is part of our spiritual breathing. We breathe in His Word and we breathe out in prayer. God talks to us through His Word by His Spirit within us. We talk to Him through prayer. We should pray to have a deepening ongoing relationship with God. The more we talk to Him, and the more we hear from Him through His Spirit and word, the deeper our relationship with Him will become.

One obvious time for us to pray is when we have struggled with sin. The response is a prayer of confession.

> *"If we confess our sins, he is faithful and just to forgive us our sins and to cleanse us from all unrighteousness."*
> *I John 1:9*

He forgives our sins, and he cleanses us from obligation to repay the debt of that sin. He sets us free.

Another area for prayer is when we are worried or anxious.

> "do not be anxious about anything, but in everything by prayer and supplication with thanksgiving let your requests be made known to God. And the peace of God, which surpasses all understanding, will guard your hearts and your minds in Christ Jesus."
> Philippians 4:6-7

Prayer brings peace. We all need the peace that only God can give, especially when we are anxious or worried.

We should pray for wisdom when we are unsure of God's will.

> "If anyone lacks wisdom, he should ask God who gives generously without finding fault, and it will be given him."
> James 1:5

Prayer is not as much to align God with our wishes as it is to align us with His will. The peace of God comes when we are still before Him and recognize that it is us who are wanting to rush around and get stuff done.

We are all a little too much like Martha and not enough like Mary, who sat at Jesus' feet. When we rest in God's promises and provisions, He brings us great peace.

"Whatever you ask in my name, this I will do, that the Father may be glorified in the Son. 14 If you ask me anything in my name, I will do it."
John 14:13-14

MORE VERSES FOR FURTHER STUDY AND REFLECTION

I John 5:14-15   Mark 11:24
I Chronicles 16:11   Psalm 17:6
Ephesians 6:18   Matthew 7:11
Jeremiah 29:12

CHAPTER 16

BIBLE STUDY

"Your word is a lamp unto my feet and a light unto my path."
Psalm 119:105

"Blessed is the man who walks not in the counsel of the wicked, nor stands in the way of sinners, nor sits in the seat of scoffers, but his delight is in the law of the Lord, and on his law he meditates day and night. He is like a tree planted by streams of water that yields its fruit in its season, and its leaf does not wither. In all that he does, he prospers."
Psalm 1:1-3

In the last chapter, we learned how prayer is part of our spiritual breathing. Prayer is our exhale, and God's Word is our inhale. We also learned that the most successful prayer life also includes the Word of God.

As we know the Word of God, we are able to know God. As we learn in this chapter, the importance of God's Word and its place in our lives, my greatest hope is that we will not look at God's Word mainly as a resource to have a better life. Rather, I hope that we would see the chief result of understanding God's Word is to KNOW HIM!

In the previous chapter on the Word of God we learned about the significance that *The Bible* is truly the Word of God. We also learned that there are five basic ways to grasp the Word of God. We can read, listen, study, memorize, and meditate on the Word of God. This chapter is specifically focused on the study of God's word.

The method of Bible Study that has most greatly affected my life was taught by Howard Hendricks at Dallas Theological Seminary. Hendricks' method is based on three stages; observation, interpretation, and application.

OBSERVATION

The observation stage answers the question, "What does it say?" This is the stage in which we look at the language used to answer the questions, Who? What? When? Where? and How?

This stage is an investigation of the details of the verse—in the same way an investigator looks intently at a crime scene to determine all the facts. The more facts that are assessed, the better the accumulation of the facts will lead to greater and deeper answers. Too often in Christianity we think we are not to ask too many questions. In this stage of Bible study, the more questions you ask the more answers you will find.

Often, we must also look into the context of the verse or verses we are studying to get the bigger picture of what is going on in the verse.

For example, we can look at James 1 and believe that we must work for our salvation, yet in the context of the book we realize that James wrote it to those who were already Christians. He was writing to them to explain how to live out their faith. We must study the Word of God in context.

INTERPRETATION

The interpretation stage answers the question, "What does it Mean?" This is the stage in which we take all of the observations and put them together to see what they mean. We can take two, three, or more word phrases and see what they mean based on our observations.

Once we have a good understanding of the meaning of the phrases, we can put them together to see what the entire verse means. A great way to insure a Biblical interpretation is to cross reference our interpretation with other sections of scripture. Nothing interprets scripture like scripture.

Most Bibles will have these cross references noted in the middle of the page, or at the bottom of each page. Don't forget to utilize the context of both the verse you are studying and the verses that you cross reference.

An additional way to ensure good interpretation of scripture is to do a word study. *The Bible* was originally written in Greek, Hebrew, and Chaldean. There are many tools that we can use to take the word or phrase back to the original language and investigate what the individual word means. There are often synonyms listed that can help in our understanding of the word usage in the verse.

Another step I sometimes take when I am still unsure of an interpretation of a section of scripture is to turn to those who have also studied in depth the verses I am studying. For example, I can turn to commentaries from Godly men who I trust in their doctrine.

Reading commentaries from authors or pastors is not my first option—this is a backup option that is great for comparing the interpretation that the

Holy Spirit leads me to through in-depth study and that which He has done in others.

APPLICATION

The application stage answers the question, "What do I Do?" This is the stage in which we put feet to our understanding. Generally, this stage gives us clarity about the steps we should take in response to the Holy Spirit's leading in Gods' word. A helpful acronym that Howard Hendricks came up with is SPECK.

Is there a **Sin** that we should confess?

Is there a **Promise** that we should claim?

Is there an **Example** to follow?

Is there a **Command** to obey?

Is there **Knowledge** about God, us, or others to learn?

A great way to understand the application stage is to write down a single sentence that represents your response to the Bible Study that day. Maybe we should even put that application sentence on a notecard with the verse written on the other side and carry it with us as a constant reminder of what God shows us each day.

An additional step in the application stage would be to share our application sentence with a close friend or mentor and ask them to hold us accountable to actually apply it to our lives.

GOSPEL

This stage is not one of the timeless treasures taught by Howard Hendricks at Dallas Theological Seminary. I include this stage in the application stage, although it is listed as an additional stage in this chapter.

The Gospel stage answers the question, "What about the Gospel?" This is the stage in which we look deeper into the verses content and context to see if and how this section of scripture points us to a greater need than application of a Biblical truth to our lives. The greatest need in the life of a not-yet believer, as well as for a believer, is the Gospel.

Therefore, we must include The Gospel in every aspect of the Christian walk. In this stage we look at the verses to see if there is a broader view that points us to the cross of Christ.

For example, in the story of the prodigal son (Luke 15:11-32), we can all see how this mirrors God's love and forgiveness for us. The son who has wasted all the Father has blessed us with, yet when we realize it and run back to our Heavenly Father, He accepts us with open arms. However, many of us miss the elder son and the picture of Jesus we gain from further investigation into him.

The younger brother took half of the future inheritance that would one day be his, therefore, everything left over would one day be the elder brother's possession. When we see the younger brother return, the father puts a robe and a ring on him and kills the fattened calf in celebration that this child of his who left him has returned. Who did the robe, ring, and calf belong to?

Yes, it was the elder brother's. The elder brother who obeyed his father's will, stayed beside his father, and did that which was expected and asked of him. Yet, it was at the cost of his inheritance that the younger brother was accepted and reconciled into the family. Our elder brother is Jesus, who obeyed his father's will, stayed beside his father, and did that which was expected and asked of him. He then paid a great price so that all his younger brothers could be reconciled unto his father.

An additional step in the Gospel stage is to apply the Gospel to the application we learned. If there is a sin pointed out for us to confess, we must believe that in the Gospel of Jesus Christ that Jesus paid the price of our sin debt and that as we trust in Jesus' sacrifice on the cross we can be forgiven.

As we seek to apply God's word to our lives, we will realize the weaknesses we have to obey. As we understand the Gospel on a deeper level, we will realize that those who know the God of the Bible personally run to him when they sin instead of running and hiding from him.

We do this act of running to God because we know that he loves us, is kind to us, is merciful and full of grace.

If we skip this step of applying the Gospel to our Bible Study we can end up just landing on condemnation instead of repentance.

> *"Therefore, there is now no condemnation for those in Christ Jesus."*
> *Romans 8:1*

We can also not understand our weaknesses and need for accountability and an avenue of repentance when we discover how much we fail.

HOW TO HAVE A BIBLE STUDY PLAN

We must have a plan if we are going to have a lifestyle of studying *The Bible*. It will not just happen. We will not just all of a sudden pick up our Bibles at random times and dive deep into it to study the precepts and applications of the Word of God to our lives unless we have a plan.

This Bible Study plan begins with answering some minor questions. When are we going to study *The Bible*? What time of day will we study? Where are we going to study—at a desk, in a park, in a closet, breakfast bar, kitchen table, in our bed, etc.

What part of *The Bible* are we going to study? These questions are important to answer in order to have a good Bible study plan.

The best time and place to have the study is when and where you can focus and be alone.

There is no best place to start in *The Bible*. In my experience, I have found that for the appropriate context, it is better to study one book of *The Bible* at a time. Start in the beginning of a book and walk through the Bible study method verse by verse, chapter by chapter.

This method will ensure that you will never run out of things to study. Many people think that they need someone else's book about a book of *The Bible* in order to study *The Bible*. These can be helpful, but they allow the Holy Spirit to teach you with individual study first.

Set a time, a place, a book of *The Bible* to begin with, and then begin.

HOW DO I BEGIN?

I begin by having my bible, pen, or pencil, and something to write on. I keep these items in the place that I want to meet with God in His Word. Pray that God would close your mind to everything else around you so that He can give you great focus to hear from Him in His Word. Pray that the Holy Spirit will reveal the depths of truth from God for you, for today.

Come to *The Bible* expecting to hear from God. Open *The Bible* to the section of scripture that you have decided to study. Read *The Bible* aloud. Read it and listen to it.

Now, write the verses you are going to study on paper with the verse references. Walk through the steps described in this chapter—observation, interpretation, application, and Gospel. Once you have walked through each of these stages, write down the statement of what you believe that God showed you. Finish by committing what God has done in you by prayer. REPEAT!

> *"Taste and See that the Lord is Good, blessed is the man who takes refuge in Him."*
> *Psalm 34:8*

MORE VERSES FOR FURTHER STUDY AND REFLECTION

II Timothy 3:14-17
Joshua 1:8
Proverbs 3:5-6
John 8:32
Jeremiah 15:16
II Peter 1:3-4
Psalm 19:7-11

CHAPTER 17

CHURCH

"The early Christian church had no buildings, at least not in the sense of what we would consider church buildings today. First century Christians were often persecuted and, as a result, often met in secret usually in homes. As the influence of Christianity spread, eventually buildings dedicated to worship were established and became what we know today as churches. In this sense, then, the church consists of people not buildings. Fellowship, worship, and ministry are all conducted by people, not buildings. Church structures facilitate the role of God's people, but they do not fulfill it."

Robert Velarde in his Focus on the Family broadcast, "What is the Church?" (Velarde, n.d.)

> *"And they devoted themselves to the apostles' teaching and the fellowship, to the breaking of bread and the prayers. 43 And awe came upon every soul, and many wonders and signs were being done through the apostles. 44 And all who believed were together and had all things in common. 45 And they were selling their possessions and belongings and distributing the proceeds to all, as any had need. 46 And day by day, attending the temple together and breaking bread in their homes, they received their food with glad and generous hearts, 47 praising God and having favor with all the people. And the Lord added to their number day by day those who were being saved."*
> *Acts 2:42-47*

Worship - in verse 43, "And Awe came upon every soul..."

The act of being in awe is worship. It is the feeling that someone much greater than you is in your presence. Worship is often described as being full of awe. Also in verse 42, *"...devoted themselves to the apostles' teaching and the fellowship, to the breaking of bread and the prayers."* The breaking of bread signifies the Lord's Supper, the sacrament of remembrance of Jesus' body being broken, and His blood being spilled out for the forgiveness of sins.

The Lords' Supper is signified throughout the breaking of bread and drinking of wine/ juice from the vine in remembrance of Jesus' last supper with his disciples. Also in verse 46, *"And day by day, attending the temple together and breaking bread in their homes,..."*.

Instruction - in verse 42, *"And they devoted themselves to the apostles teaching..."* This act of devoting themselves to the teachings of the apostles shows that when they gathered together there was very clear instruction from God. The instruction was not simply a hearing of the word, but a doing of the word, hence the term "devoted themselves."

Fellowship - in verse 42, *"And they devoted themselves to the apostles' teaching and to fellowship, the breaking of bread and the prayers."* They clearly were devoted to fellowship with one another and the breaking of bread—which is a form of fellowship both with God in worship and fellowship and those with whom we share the sacrament. In verse 44 and 45, *"And all who believed were* *together and had all things in common. And they were selling their possessions and belongings and distributing the proceeds to all, as any had need."*

These verses show some of the evidence of the truest forms of fellowship; together, had things in common, giving, providing, and together "day by day" in verse 46. Also, they did this with glad and generous hearts, in verse 46. Also, *"having favor with all the people"* in verse 47.

Evangelism - in verse 47, *"And the Lord added to their number day by day those who were being saved."* For people to be saved, the Gospel (the life, death, burial, and resurrection of Jesus Christ) must be shared.

Evangelism is the sharing of the gospel of Jesus Christ in the power of the Holy Spirit and then leaving the results to God.

This result in verse 47 of people being saved day by day demonstrates results that could only come about by the Gospel being evident in the daily proclamation of the believers to not-yet believers.

THE GREAT COMMISSION OF THE CHURCH

"And Jesus came and said to them, All authority in heaven and on

*earth has been given to me. 19 Go
therefore and make disciples of all
nations, baptizing them in[a] the name
of the Father and of the Son and of
the Holy Spirit, 20 teaching them to
observe all that I have commanded
you. And behold, I am with you
always, to the end of the age."*
                Matthew 28:18-19

The chief call of the church is to "make disciples of all nations." Sadly, this is often the last thing the church does.

The church does a great job of helping people belong to a community of people, finding niches of needs in the community through feeding the hungry, clothing the naked, providing homes for homeless, creating programs for all ages of people in their church demographic makeup, and having weekly, bi-weekly and even daily activities for its members. However, the biggest weakness of the church is sadly its greatest calling—to make disciples.

*"And the things you've heard
me say in the presence of many
witnesses, entrust to reliable men,*

who will also be qualified to teach others."
II Timothy 2:2

"Discipling is the process by which a Christian with a life worth emulating commits himself for an extended period of time to a few individuals who have been won to Christ, the purpose being to aid and guide their growth to spiritual maturity and to equip them to reproduce themselves into a third spiritual generation."
Allen Hadidian, Discipleship-Helping Other Christians Grow (Hadidian, 1987)

In this book, there are 7 chapters dedicated to discipleship—what it is, how we can do it, etc. In fact, this entire book is about discipleship. The chapters that do not directly deal with discipleship are the areas in verse 20, *"teaching them to observe all that I have commanded you."*

SACRAMENTS OF THE LORD'S SUPPER AND BAPTISM

The Lord's Supper and Baptism are the sacraments of the church. These are the Holy and worshipful activities that take place on a regular basis in Christian churches to point us to Jesus and our permanent need for Him.

The Lord's Supper points us to the constant need for repentance and faith as we are instructed to reconcile to God and others prior to partaking in the bread and wine (juice of the vine). The bread represents the body of Christ broken for you, and the wine represents the blood that poured out of Jesus on Calvary's cross for you and me and the forgiveness of our sins.

This sacrament reminds us of the body and blood of Jesus Christ that was broken and poured out for us on the cross for our sins. This sacrament is an ongoing reminder of our need of Jesus and promotes repentance of our sins and further placement of our faith in the person and finished work of Jesus Christ for us.

Baptism is the sacrament that displays the work of Christ to wash away our sins, or the display of Christ having already washed away our sins. There are baptisms that are for those who have already repented of their sins to God for forgiveness and placed their faith in Jesus Christ, trusting in his finished work on the cross for salvation.

These baptisms for believers are called Believers Baptism. There are also covenantal baptisms. These are equally sacraments that are Holy and worshipful. The covenantal baptism can occur in infants who have not yet placed their faith in Jesus Christ.

These baptisms are a sign of the covenant that God has made with the believing parent or parents that they will raise the child in a home where the Gospel is taught and displayed in the hopes that God will bring them to faith in Jesus Christ in the future.

In both baptisms, there is a need of evidence or future evidence that there is a lifestyle of repentance and faith for those in the church to believe that they have become believers in Christ. There will be those who were baptized as believers baptism who never truly placed their faith in Jesus Christ.

There will also be those who were covenantally baptized whose parents raised them in the Gospel, but whom never truly place their faith in Jesus Christ. The sacrament does not save the person's soul. Only Jesus Saves.

THE CHURCH LEADERSHIP

The head of the church is Jesus Christ. There are several versions of church leadership. There are churches that are led by a pastor/shepherd with other leaders who assist in the leadership of the church. Those leaders may be called elders or deacons or pastors or leadership team, etc.

There is also leadership by elders and deacons of the church, wherein the pastor is the lead teaching elder of the church.

The church may have paid staff who serve in either role of elder or deacon. The paid staff may serve in specific ministry needs of the church, for example, children, youth, college, seniors, small groups, missions, evangelism, discipleship, education, executive needs, etc.

Elders are responsible for protecting the vision, passion, and purity of the church. Elders are committed to knowing the members well enough to lead them in their journey spiritually, emotionally, mentally, financially, as well as physically. The elders are responsible for feeding the members spiritually.

They are able to teach the truths of *The Bible*, whether it be one-on-one or small groups.

The elders are also responsible for protecting the members from false doctrines and relationally. Each elder should go through extensive training in leadership and discipleship and be equipped to make disciples, to counsel, to lead, and to teach.

They all must meet the Biblical requirements expressed in I Timothy 3:1-13.

"Here is a trustworthy saying: Whoever aspires to be an overseer desires a noble task. 2 Now the overseer is to be above reproach, faithful to his wife, temperate, self-controlled, respectable, hospitable, able to teach, 3 not given to drunkenness, not violent but gentle, not quarrelsome, not a lover of money. 4 He must manage his own family well and see that his children obey him, and he must do so in a manner worthy of full respect. 5 (If anyone does not know how to manage his own family, how can he take care of God's church?) 6 He must not be a recent convert, or he

*may become conceited and fall under
the same judgment as the devil. 7 He
must also have a good reputation with
outsiders, so that he will not fall into
disgrace and into the devil's trap.8 In
the same way, deacons are to be
worthy of respect, sincere, not
indulging in much wine, and not
pursuing dishonest gain. 9 They must
keep hold of the deep truths of the
faith with a clear conscience. 10 They
must first be tested; and then if there
is nothing against them, let them
serve as deacons.11 In the same
way, the women are to be worthy of
respect, not malicious talkers but
temperate and trustworthy in
everything.12 A deacon must be
faithful to his wife and must manage
his children and his household well.
13 Those who have served well gain
an excellent standing and great
assurance in their faith in Christ
Jesus."*
I Timothy 3:1-13

The requirements are also found in Titus 1:5-
9.

"The reason I left you in Crete was that you might put in order what was left unfinished and appoint elders in every town, as I directed you. 6 An elder must be blameless, faithful to his wife, a man whose children believe and are not open to the charge of being wild and disobedient. 7 Since an overseer manages God's household, he must be blameless—not overbearing, not quick-tempered, not given to drunkenness, not violent, not pursuing dishonest gain. 8 Rather, he must be hospitable, one who loves what is good, who is self-controlled, upright, holy and disciplined. 9 He must hold firmly to the trustworthy message as it has been taught, so that he can encourage others by sound doctrine and refute those who oppose it. are responsible to lead in the areas of building, budgets, relationship counseling and reconciliation, as well as mercy ministry."

Titus 1:5-9

Deacons are committed to knowing the members well enough to lead them to ways that they can serve the church according to their gifts and talents.

Deacons are mature believers who can articulate their faith with great clarity. Deacons must also meet the Biblical requirements expressed in I Timothy 3:1-13 and Titus 1:5-9.

There are different types of leadership in churches. There are pastor-led churches, staff-led churches, board of director-led churches, elder-led churches, etc.

Elder-led churches have a group of elders who lead the vision, passion, and purity of the church. They come together to pray, discuss, and vote on the decisions of the church.

There is great wisdom to be found in a team of leaders rather than one man.

"Without counsel plans fail, but with many advisers they succeed."
Proverbs 15:22

"Where there is no guidance, a people falls, but in an abundance of counselors there is safety."
Proverbs 11:14

YOU AND THE CHURCH

It is a sad, sad statement when I mention the evangelistic focus of our church is the unchurched and the de-churched. The unchurched seems self explanatory. The de-churched may seem a bit confusing. For the most part, this group of people still love the Jesus of *The Bible*.

They may even have some clear disciplines of grace who are manifested in their lives; bible study, prayer, fellowship, evangelism, etc.

They look like other Christians, yet they have just been burned badly by the local church—by a staff member, leader, member, or even just had a certain preference that was overlooked.

The feeling and the actions that have been endured by the de-churched are real. I know the feeling. I understand being overlooked, not appreciated, or feeling like I have been ignored. Or, much worse. In the following statement, Trudy Smith expresses this well:

> *"I realized that church was not a place to go because everyone had their act together. It was more like a refuge where all sorts of people could gather to remind each other of the story we are all in. ... So I've slowly*

learned that going to church can be about something other than moral requirement, fear of punishment, social connection, getting spiritually fed, or even looking for likeminded people with whom to pursue justice in the world. Going to church can be about holding this space in which to experience the grace of God together, learn together, fail and forgive, and stumble forward together."

("Why I Go To Church Even When I Don't Feel Like It," by Trudy Smith, Relevant Magazine, September 8, 2015 (Smith, 2015)

"Let us hold fast the confession of our hope without wavering, for he who promised is faithful. 24 And let us consider how to stir up one another to love and good works, 25 not neglecting to meet together, as is the habit of some, but encouraging one another, and all the more as you see the Day drawing near."

Hebrews 10:23-25

Attending and/or joining a local church is a big decision that is difficult for many to make. Realize that some may say, "Well I don't need the church. All it has done is hurt me." Please realize that the church needs you, and there are people in the local church who need to learn from your pain, as well.

"And he gave the apostles, the prophets, the evangelists, the shepherds and teachers, 12 to equip the saints for the work of ministry, for building up the body of Christ, 13 until we all attain to the unity of the faith and of the knowledge of the Son of God, to mature manhood, to the measure of the stature of the fullness of Christ, 14 so that we may no longer be children, tossed to and fro by the waves and carried about by every wind of doctrine, by human cunning, by craftiness in deceitful schemes. 15 Rather, speaking the truth in love, we are to grow up in every way into him who is the head, into Christ, 16 from whom the whole body, joined and held together by every joint with which it is equipped, when each part is

working properly, makes the body
grow so that it builds itself up in love."
Ephesians 4:11-16

You were designed for community. The church community needs you. Your gifts and talents were given to you by God to be used for his Glory in the Body of Christ.

MORE VERSES FOR FURTHER STUDY AND REFLECTION

Hebrews 10:24-25
Isaiah 62:12
Hebrews 3:6
Romans12:4-5
I Corinthians 3:9
Ephesians 4:12-16
Colossians 3:14-16

CHAPTER 18

FELLOWSHIP

No relationship will be as deep as your relationship with God. However, every relationship will be deeper because of your relationship with God.

When a man or a woman has a deep personal relationship with God, their capacity to love others is magnified. When we understand how God forgives, we are enabled to forgive much more. When we experience God's compassion toward us, we gain compassion for others. The key to having deep fellowship with one another is to have deep fellowship with God.

"And they devoted themselves to the apostles' teaching and the fellowship, to the breaking of bread and the prayers. 43 And awe came upon every soul, and many wonders and signs were being done through the apostles. 44 And all who believed were together and had all things in common. 45 And they were selling their possessions and belongings and distributing the proceeds to all, as any

*had need. **46** And day by day,*
attending the temple together and
breaking bread in their homes, they
received their food with glad and
*generous hearts, **47** praising God and*
having favor with all the people. And
the Lord added to their number day by
day those who were being saved."
Acts 2:42-47

They devoted themselves to fellowship. This is not a haphazard ideal that happens at random. It is a devotion. It is action that requires intentionality. We must be purposeful in how we spend time together. We can spend time with other believers and it not be fellowship. Fellowship with believers is based on what holds us together—which is Christ.

They devoted themselves to the breaking of bread and the prayers. This communicates that they were also devoted to spiritual practices, such as the Lord's Supper and also to praying together and for one another.

All who believed were together and had all things in common. They looked for the good in each other. They found the similarities in their life situations, and they were together. The early believers in *The Bible* were a team working together for each other. They had common goals, directions, struggles, and ways to cope with each obstacle. They lived life together in community with one another.

They were selling their possessions and belonging and distributing to all who had need. They looked out for the needs of one another. When one struggled, they all came together. When someone needed something, that need was met within the group. They were not simply physically gathered together often. They were together in this calling to live like Christ. They did not simply look out for their own needs, but they attended to the needs of others. They had to know one another on a deep level to recognize the needs and to be able to know which needs were present.

Day by day they worshipped God and had meals together with glad and generous hearts. This act of being together was not a job—it was a pleasure. They were happy to be together. Their glad and generous hearts can easily be linked to the fact that they worshipped God instead of themselves. When we worship God we see how generous He is to us, and it overflows through us to others.

They were praising God and having favor with all the people. They were not looking for the things that were lacking in their lives. They were looking at the things they could be thankful for and praising God for them. They were having favor with all people. This meant that they also were not looking at each other to complain about each other's weaknesses, but rather they were looking at what they could be thankful for in one another. Praising God causes a gratefulness in us that looks for the good in his people, as well.

As we read about this fellowship in Acts, Chapter 2, some of us develop a growing desire to experience this for the first time. Others have had this kind of fellowship before, and still others do not believe it is possible. In our own effort, it is truly impossible. In our own strength, we will not look to others' interests—only to our own.

We are naturally selfish. This begins at an early age. Look at any child who has a new friend come to their room and listen how many times we hear them yell, "Mine!" We do not naturally share our love, life, or belongings with others. To love this way takes a super natural work in us by the Holy Spirit. His work in us is ongoing. What he began in us he will continue.

"We can pray being confident of this that He who began a good work in you will continue it to

*completion until the day of Christ
Jesus."*
Philippians 1:6

*"So then just as you received
Christ Jesus as Lord, so continue in
Him, rooted and built up in him,
strengthened in the faith as you were
taught and overflowing with
thanksgiving."*
Colossians 2:6-7

Another area of fellowship that is often overlooked is that we are not only to share our fellowship with God with each other, but we should also share our lives.

*"Just as a nursing mother
cares for her children, **8** so we cared
for you we cared for you. Because we
loved you so much, we were delighted
to share with you not only the gospel
of God but our lives as well."*
I Thessalonians 2:7-8

*"For you know that we dealt
with each of you as a father deals with
his own children, 12 encouraging,
comforting and urging you to live lives
worthy of God, who calls you into his
kingdom and glory."*
I Thessalonians 2:11-12

Biblical fellowship is much like family. The depth of the relationships with the Family of God can often be as deep as your blood relationships. Many of the Family of God relationships can be even deeper than those of our immediate family.

Yet another area of fellowship is praying for one another.

*"Therefore, confess your sins
to one another, and pray for one
another so that you may be healed
the effective prayer of a righteous
man can accomplish much."*
James 5:16

Literally, here it says that by going to our brother or sister in Christ and confessing sin and praying for one another that you may be healed. Many of us have ailments that have plagued us.

Others view this as sins that have plagued us. We have victory in Jesus Christ. We can go to Him in prayer together and beseech Him to deliver our brother or sister in Christ in specific areas that they have felt confident enough in our fellowship with them to confess to us.

Lastly, when we don't fellowship with one another the way that God intended we weaken the entire body of Christ.

> "Just as a body, though one, has many parts, but all its many parts form one body, so it is with Christ. 13 For we were all baptized by one Spirit so as to form one body— whether Jews or Gentiles, slave or free—and we were all given the one Spirit to drink. 14 Even so the body is not made up of one part but of many. 15 Now if the foot should say, "Because I am not a hand, I do not belong to the body," it would not for that reason stop being part of the body. 16 And if the ear should say, "Because I am not an eye, I do not belong to the body," it would not for that reason stop being part of the

body. *17 If the whole body were an eye, where would the sense of hearing be? If the whole body were an ear, where would the sense of smell be? 18 But in fact God has placed the parts in the body, every one of them, just as he wanted them to be. 19 If they were all one part, where would the body be? 20 As it is, there are many parts, but one body.*

21 The eye cannot say to the hand, "I don't need you!" And the head cannot say to the feet, "I don't need you!" 22 On the contrary, those parts of the body that seem to be weaker are indispensable, 23 and the parts that we think are less honorable we treat with special honor. And the parts that are unpresentable are treated with special modesty, 24 while our presentable parts need no special treatment. But God has put the body together, giving greater honor to the parts that lacked it, 25 so that there should be no division in the body, but that its parts should have equal concern for each other. 26 If one part suffers, every part suffers with it; if

one part is honored, every part
rejoices with it."
I Corinthians 12:12-26

We are each part of the Body of Christ. When we are not being who God made us to be as part of the body, the whole body suffers. We need you in the Body of Christ. We need you in deep fellowship with God and with your brothers and sisters.

"So Christ himself gave the apostles, the prophets, the evangelists, the pastors and teachers, 12 to equip his people for works of service, so that the body of Christ may be built up 13 until we all reach unity in the faith and in the knowledge of the Son of God and become mature, attaining to the whole measure of the fullness of Christ.

14 Then we will no longer be infants, tossed back and forth by the waves, and blown here and there by every wind of teaching and by the cunning and craftiness of people in their deceitful scheming. 15 Instead, speaking the truth in love, we will

*grow to become in every respect the
mature body of him who is the head,
that is, Christ. **16** From him the whole
body, joined and held together by
every supporting ligament, grows and
builds itself up in love, as each part
does its work."*
                    Ephesians 4:11-16

We need you in the Body of Christ, and we
need you in deep fellowship with us. In addition, we
need you to discover, develop, and to exercise your
gifts with the Body of Christ.

MORE VERSES FOR FURTHER STUDY AND
REFLECTION

Ecclesiastes 4:9-12
Hebrews 10:24
Proverbs 27:17
Philippians 2:1-5
I John 4:7
John 15-12
John 13:34

CHAPTER 19

EVANGELISM

"If you declare with your mouth, "Jesus is Lord," and believe in your heart that God raised him from the dead, you will be saved. 10 For it is with your heart that you believe and are justified, and it is with your mouth that you profess your faith and are saved. 11 As Scripture says, "Anyone who believes in him will never be put to shame." 12 For there is no difference between Jew and Gentile— the same Lord is Lord of all and richly blesses all who call on him, 13 for, "Everyone who calls on the name of the Lord will be saved."
Romans 10:9-13

Evangelism is proclaiming the truths about Jesus Christ—His life, death, burial, and resurrection. We will be discussing each of these truths in this chapter, however, we must also understand the call to share these truths and practical ways to earn an audience with whom these truths should be shared.

> *"How, then, can they call on the one they have not believed in? And how can they believe in the one of whom they have not heard? And how can they hear without someone preaching to them? 15 And how can anyone preach unless they are sent? As it is written: "How beautiful are the feet of those who bring good news!"*
> Romans 10:14-15

Often, I am asked, "What about that good guy in Africa who has never heard about Jesus?" My response always begins with the idea that if you are burdened for a guy in Africa, when are you going to Africa to tell him. I then explain the issues with the question.

The first is that there isn't a good guy in Africa who has never heard about Jesus because there isn't a good guy in Africa, or anywhere for that matter. Second, this question usually has nothing to do with someone in Africa needing to understand what Jesus has done for them. Rather, it is an excuse not to share the truths about Jesus with anyone. Third, an additional reason to ask this question is to try to discount the value of Jesus' life, death, burial, and resurrection in that there are other ways to God.

In the Garden of Gethsemane Jesus prayed to God, "If *there be any other way, take this cup from me.*" As the guards seize him, Peter cuts off one of his ears, and Jesus says to Peter, "*shall I not drink from the cup the father has given me.*" Peter is clearing up the matter at hand. He asked God that if there was any other way to a relationship with God to take the cup from Him. After praying, God clarified that there is no other way than for Jesus to die on the cross for our sins. We must tell everyone! No excuses!

> *"Salvation is found in no one else, for there is no other name under heaven given to mankind by which we must be saved."*
> *Acts 4:12*

God has saved us and adopted us into the family, in order to use us as his messengers of salvation to all mankind.

"All this is from God, who reconciled us to himself through Christ and gave us the ministry of reconciliation: 19 that God was reconciling the world to himself in Christ, not counting people's sins against them. And he has committed to us the message of reconciliation. 20 We are therefore Christ's ambassadors, as though God were making his appeal through us. We implore you on Christ's behalf: Be reconciled to God. 21 God made him who had no sin to be sin for us, so that in him we might become the righteousness of God."

II Corinthians 5:18-21

HOW DO WE EARN THE RIGHT TO SPEAK INTO PEOPLE'S LIVES?

We see Jesus often meet needs in people's lives, and then we tell them about eternal life. He heals people, feeds people, blesses people, talks with people about their problems, listens to people, teaches people, and even performs miracles in front of them. He then explains the truths about himself. Our methods should follow our model. We should evangelize the way that Jesus did.

I believe that evangelism includes the hands, feet, and mouth of Jesus. The hands and feet are blessing people in service or needs that they have and living out the truths of *The Bible* in front of them. The mouth of Jesus is to tell people about Him.

I had a neighbor who was going through a divorce. He was struggling. I saw him doing work in his yard one day, so I joined him. I just asked him how things were going. He paused and asked, "How do you and your wife keep your relationship together so well?" Think about how you would answer that question.

Now think about how to use that question as a way to transition the conversation to speak about Jesus. I answered him with the truth, "We don't." He said, "What do you mean?" I said, "If our relationship success was determined by our ability to hold it together it would be doomed to failure." He replied, "What holds your relationship together then?" I spent the next 30 minutes telling him about Jesus Christ's life, death, burial, and resurrection and how it applies to our lives and marriage. How do you think he left that conversation? Amazed by two Christians? Or amazed by Jesus Christ?

Another way that we can ensure opportunities to speak into people's lives is to be in people's lives. There is no impact without contact.

HOW DOES ANYONE HAVE TIME FOR EVANGELISM?

How can we not have time to share the most important message of our lives with other people? Everyone uses every hour of every day for something. It may be for a nap, or on things that are a waste of time, but we still use every hour. I know that we can't add hours to the day, and for most people we can't add any more activities to our busy schedules. I am not talking about adding more activities.

Rather, I am going to introduce a new mentality. We are the image bearers of God everywhere we go. We have conversations with people every day. We meet people every week. We need to live with Gospel intentionality. We take the Gospel of Jesus Christ with us everywhere we go. Let's take it on purpose for the purpose of proclaiming Him.

A few ideas that you can use and add to for your context of life. I eat at the same restaurants with the same waiter or waitress. I go into the bank to make deposits, and I talk with people about life, not just business. I invite neighbors to our home for cookouts. I allow my children to have friends in our home from our neighborhood and their school often. We coordinate activities in our schools, neighborhoods, and city just to love them well and show them we care.

I don't eat in public alone. I rarely travel anywhere alone if I can help it. I take people with me. I volunteer to coach my kids' sports teams. I play on sports teams in adult leagues.

I have been blessed with the opportunity to see people come to faith in Jesus Christ while I shared The Gospel with them—when they called the wrong number and I answered, in a car wreck with me that was my fault, on the beach playing volleyball, at a carnival, on a plane sitting next to me, at work, driving around on a golf cart, in a sports gymnasium, on the front lawn of my house, on a construction site, at a soccer game, in their home writing a sales contract on their house while representing the buyer, in a fraternity house, in my garage, in a horse barn, in my office, in the middle of marriage counseling, after a music concert, at a junk yard, in a restaurant . . . and there are more. These are just examples. How can you have Gospel intentionality in your life? With whom do you already talk? Who are you going to talk to next?

WHAT DO I SAY?

Chapter 9 demonstrated an effective method called the Bridge Diagram. I have used this for many years to explain The Gospel.

> *"Now, brothers and sisters, I want to remind you of the gospel I preached to you, which you received and on which you have taken your stand. 2 By this gospel you are saved, if you hold firmly to the word I preached to you. Otherwise, you have believed in vain.*
>
> *3 For what I received I passed on to you as of first importance: that Christ died for our sins according to the Scriptures, 4 that he was buried, that he was raised on the third day according to the Scriptures, 5 and that he appeared to Cephas, and then to the Twelve. 6 After that, he appeared to more than five hundred of the brothers and sisters at the same time, most of whom are still living, though some have fallen asleep."*
>
> *I Corinthians 15:1-6*

The Gospel is what we say. The life, death, burial, and resurrection of Jesus Christ. Jesus lived the perfect life that none of us could live, and then he died the brutal death that none of us want to die. He died in our place on the cross to pay the debt we owed God because of sin.

"For the wages of sin is death, but the gift of God is eternal life through Christ Jesus our Lord."
Romans 6:23

He became our substitutionary sacrifice. He took our place, so that we could take his place.

"God made him who knew no sin, to be sin for us, so that we might become the righteousness of God."
II Corinthians 5:21

"For I am not ashamed of the gospel, because it is the power of God that brings salvation to everyone who believes: first to the Jew, then to the Gentile."
Romans 1:16

MORE VERSES FOR FURTHER STUDY AND REFLECTION

Acts 13:47

Mark 16:15

Acts 20:24

Psalm 105:1

I Peter 3:15

Mark 8:35

Acts 1:8

CHAPTER 20

DISCIPLESHIP MEETINGS

In the first seven chapters, discipleship was explained. This chapter is the practical application of what to do in the discipleship meetings. Of course, if you invest your life in your disciples there will be opportunities to teach them at all times of your interaction with them, but there also needs to be scheduled regular meetings. I will discuss both in this chapter.

> *"Let us hold unswervingly to the hope we profess, for he who promised is faithful. 24 And let us consider how we may spur one another on toward love and good deeds, 25 not giving up meeting together, as some are in the habit of doing, but encouraging one another— and all the more as you see the Day approaching."*
> *Hebrews 10:23-25*

We must live life on life in front of them. This concept is explained in Chapter 21. We must model for and train our disciples in the attitudes and actions we desire for them. Utilize teachable moments. We are basically mentoring or parenting a younger Christian in how to grow to maturity and reproduce himself.

> *"And the things you've heard*
> *me say in the presence of many*
> *witnesses, entrust to reliable men who*
> *will also be qualified to teach others."*
> *II Timothy 2:2*

Sometimes you may have a time scheduled for training with all the details mapped out in your mind and even on paper, and then once you meet with your disciple they ask a pressing question that gives a greater opportunity to train them even deeper on an area that already interests them. Be flexible in your meeting time each week.

Discipleship is not just a teaching time. It is not simply a class about *The Bible.* It is truly sharing the Gospel and your life with a few individuals to train them up in the Lord.

"so we cared for you. Because we loved you so much, we were delighted to share with you not only the gospel of God but our lives as well... For you know that we dealt with each of you as a father deals with his own children, 12 encouraging, comforting and urging you to live lives worthy of God, who calls you into his kingdom and glory."

I Thessalonians 2:8 and 2:11-12

Here are some meeting suggestions from my experience during the last 24 years. These are not meant to apply any added pressure, but rather to bring some freedom to your meeting times. Any one of the below, any combination of the below, or any other way you can lead people from where they are into a deeper walk with Jesus will be awesome.

GET TO KNOW THOSE WITH WHOM YOU ARE DISCIPLING

Ask how they became a Christian (3-5 minutes)
1. What was your life like before you were a Christian? (childhood, experience)

2. How did you understand your need for Christ?
3. How did you become a Christian?
4. What is your life like now?

Ask about their week.
1. What does your average week look like?
2. How is your time spent? (work, home life, hobbies, family, etc.)

Ask them about their walk with the Lord.
1. What has the Lord been teaching you lately?

Pray and follow up with them to see how God worked.
1. Meet with your group to share some prayer requests for their week, and then pray for those areas.
2. Ask about the topic of the week. See if they have read or discussed it yet.
3. See what parts really stood out to them. Ask why? How does this change anything?
4. Ask if there are some clear applications to their life they feel God is showing them?
5. Ask if there is anything that for which they would like to be held accountable?
6. Make accountability a part of the regular meeting time. (Have some for yourself, also.)

TRAINING TIME

1. If there is a specific skill to discuss with them? For example, Observation, Interpretation, Application from Chapter 16.
2. Ask if they have tried to do it, and if they have any questions about it.
3. Choose a verse to do it with them.
4. Ask again if they have any questions about what you just did.
5. Decide a goal for the week that applies their new skill.

NEED OF THE HOUR

1. Sometimes there may be horrific situations in the life of one of the disciples that requires attention for the whole meeting time.
2. Maybe have the entire group speak into their life, or pray for them.
3. Maybe there is a physical need should immediately be met through the group or church.

APPLICATION AS A TEAM

1. Perhaps there are very clear actions steps to follow through with the group.

2. This is Bible Doing instead of Bible Study. (help homeless, work on budget, teach life skill, recreational activity, etc.)
3. Go to one of the discipleship group members who is in need of help.

Love and lead your disciples to a deeper walk with Jesus each week and rely upon the Holy Spirit to do His part.

"Pray being confident of this, that he who began a good work in you will continue to completion until the day of Christ Jesus."
Philippians 1:6

MORE VERSES FOR FURTHER STUDY AND REFLECTION

Proverbs 27:17
Romans 12:10
James 5:16
John 13:34
Ephesians 6:4
III John 1:4
Proverbs 3:1

CHAPTER 21

LIFE ON LIFE

"As iron sharpens iron, so one person sharpens another."
Proverbs 27:17

Life on life is a term used to describe the day to day of discipleship. Too often, discipleship becomes a program or a project. The ultimate example of discipleship was Jesus with the 12 Disciples.

"One cannot examine the ministry of the Lord Jesus without seeing the emphasis He placed on discipling . . . From the very beginning, Christ's strategy of ministry centered on His men. He was always with them—teaching them, training them, encouraging them, rebuking them, and working His ministry in front

of them. . . They became the main
focus of His ministry."
Allen Hadidian, Discipleship-
Helping Other Christians Grow
(Hadidian, 1987)

The example that Jesus set for us could not limit us to a meeting once a week. It was His lifestyle to be among his men. The opportunity for teaching and training abound throughout the daily practices of life. He cared for His men. He didn't just get them through a program or some material. He invested his life into theirs.

The call to discipleship is not a call to a program, but a call to a people. The people we are called to disciple are the faithful, available, and teachable people who we know need to be discipled. We must pray for them, think of them, love them, and serve them. The cost is great, but so are the rewards. We literally get to watch God change their lives right before our eyes. In the process, God changes our lives, as well.

"But as for you, teach what
accords with sound doctrine. 2 Older
men are to be sober-minded,
dignified, self-controlled, sound in

faith, in love, and in steadfastness.
3 Older women likewise are to be
reverent in behavior, not slanderers or
slaves to much wine. They are to
teach what is good, 4 and so train the
young women to love their husbands
and children." The older in this
context does not only mean age, it
can also be the maturity in the Lord.
This is not merely a group setting
teaching time, it is also training.
Training is the practical day-to-day
application of God's word to our
hearts and behavior.
　　　　Titus 2:1-4

*　　　"On the contrary, we speak as*
those approved by God to be
entrusted with the gospel. We are not
trying to please people but God, who
tests our hearts. 5 You know we
never used flattery, nor did we put on
a mask to cover up greed—God is our
witness. 6 We were not looking for
praise from people, not from you or
anyone else, even though as apostles

of Christ we could have asserted our authority. 7 Instead, we were like young children among you. Just as a nursing mother cares for her children, 8 so we cared for you. Because we loved you so much, we were delighted to share with you not only the gospel of God but our lives as well. 9 Surely you remember, brothers and sisters, our toil and hardship; we worked night and day in order not to be a burden to anyone while we preached the gospel of God to you. 10 You are witnesses, and so is God, of how holy, righteous and blameless we were among you who believed. 11 For you know that we dealt with each of you as a father deals with his own children, 12 encouraging, comforting and urging you to live lives worthy of God, who calls you into his kingdom and glory." The training that goes on is not simply The Bible, but sharing our lives with one another. This spiritual parenting involves work. We are to encourage, comfort, urge, and take great personal care for the details of life. We share the joys and the sorrows. We pray, think, love, and serve."

I Thessalonians 2:4-12

Jesus did not merely enter his disciples into seminary classes and say that when you graduate you are ready to change the world. He spent his life with them. He invested his time with them. He worked his ministry in front of them every day for a period of three years. They were with him when He walked, when He ate, when He preached, when He showed mercy, and when He prayed. They were with Him as He walked out the details of all of His life.

"More is caught than taught."

"I'd rather see a sermon than hear one anyway."

These are some catchy phrases I have heard that reflect the need for life-on-life ministry and training. You can tell me what to do, but I understand it much better when you show me.

A METHOD OF LIFE-ON-LIFE TRAINING INVOLVES 5 KEY AREAS:

1. Do it in front of them.
2. Tell them why.
3. Show them how.
4. Do it with them.

5. Keep them going.

1. DO IT IN FRONT OF THEM.

When we do life in front of other people, they take notice. People understand better when they see an example. This format of giving people a model to follow is the best way to train them, and is true for most of life. Be the model you desire them to be. Live out the example in front of them. For my sons, I desire to be the Dad that I hope that they will be for their boys one day.

2. TELL THEM WHY.

As we model the truth of what we should do, we follow up with explaining the why we do it. The "why" is the answer to the question, "What Motivates you to do this or that?" The why is as important as all the other steps. Doing something just because you are supposed to isn't enough.

That reason will only work as you hold that person to the task everyday. We aren't trying to hold their hands for all of life. We are attempting to train them to be successful without us. When they understand the "why" for themselves they will continue the discipline and for the right reason.

3. SHOW THEM HOW.

Showing them how is the on-the-job training. This is the more practical approach to discussing and teaching the details of the task or discipline step by step.

4. DO IT WITH THEM.

Doing it with them is the idea that after modeling the activity, discussing the motivation, walking through the details of how to do it, we actually are there with them while they do it, and we do it with them. This step allows us to guide in real time while the activity is happening.

5. KEEP THEM GOING.

To keep them going in a given task we add in the step of encouragement and accountability. This will add motivation to the "why" by giving them courage to continue. We also add in the repeated life-on-life time with them and follow up to see how things are going in the given activity or discipline.

Here is an example of this process. I currently meet with a small group of men early in the morning. We meet to work out in a gym, then we go for coffee and personal Bible Study at a local coffee shop. We each have our Bibles, pen and paper. The first time we met like this was after I taught about how to have a personal Bible study in our community group.

One of the members of our group pulled me aside and told me he needed help with his personal Bible Study time. He said, "I can tell that the method you taught is the way that you do it, but I just can't quite get a handle on it. Can you teach me? Also, I am not very consistent." So I asked him when he wanted to have his personal Bible Study time. He said, "First thing in the morning." So we meet in the morning.

The first time we met I wrote down a verse, and then told him to do the same. I then walked through four steps that I teach in personal Bible Study: observation, interpretation, application, and Gospel. As I demonstrated each step in front of him, I had him write them down, as well. We did this for a couple of days. While walking through the verses we discussed,

> "Your word is a lamp to my feet
> and a light to my path."
> Psalm 119:105

We then discussed that God's word guides us through each day. Step by step as we follow Him, God directs us. I then walked very clearly through each step to be sure he understood clearly how to do it. By this time our meeting grew because he brought along a friend. We were careful to catch up his friend with the same training.

I then asked that he lead the time by pretending that he is teaching us how, and reinforced that I was there to help with any questions he had during the process. When he was confident in this discipline and pleasure of spending time alone with God in his word, I encouraged him in how well he was doing and still held him accountable to the discipline.

We no longer talk to each other as much during our personal Bible Study time about the process, because he understands well enough that we discuss the significance of the verses.

There are people around us every day who need us to invest our lives to make a difference in them. We often do not recognize the needs around us because we are so focused on our own lives.

We all need life-on-life ministry happening in our lives. We either need a mentor, or we need to be a mentor for someone.

MORE VERSES FOR FURTHER STUDY AND REFLECTION

II Timothy 2:2

Titus 2:3-5

Psalm 145:4

I Thessalonians 2:8

I Corinthians11:1

Ecclesiastes 4:10-12

Romans 15:14

CHAPTER 22

LEADERSHIP

Leadership is easy to notice. You simply look behind you to see if anyone is following. If so, then you are a leader. This doesn't mean that you are a good leader, it just means that you are a leader. Many leaders go through life without knowing whether they are a good leader.

Most leaders measure themselves by what they and their followers accomplish, whether it be tasks, growth of a business or ideal, or win in a sport, etc. True successful leaders measure themselves by the character, competency, and abilities of the ones they are leading. Therefore, good leaders develop their followers. Great leaders develop their followers into great leaders.

I am the Pastor of a church that has a system of leadership development. In this system, there are the following levels of leadership:

1. The ability to lead yourself
2. The ability to lead your family
3. The ability to lead others
4. The ability to lead groups of people
5. The ability to lead leaders
6. The ability to lead teams of leaders

According to *The Bible*, a leader is a shepherd. A shepherd does not herd sheep. A shepherd does not yell orders for his flock. A shepherd leads his sheep. A leader is to be the lead communicator, lead servant, lead example, lead teacher, lead instructor, lead in character, and have the ability to bring people along with him.

I have always loved this picture that distinguishes between a boss and a leader.

A boss focuses on things.

A leader focuses on people.

A boss does things right.

A leader does the right things.

A boss plans details.

A leader inspires his people to be the right people who make good decisions.

A boss organizes people.

A leader influences people.

A boss directs people.

A leader motivates people.

A boss controls people.
A leader builds people into leaders.

ARE YOU A LEADER?

> *"For even the Son of Man did not come to be served, but to serve, and to give his life as a ransom for many."*
> *Mark 10:35*

A leader is a servant who gives his life away to assist, guide, and develop his men. Leadership is all about attitude. Our preoccupation with what we deserve, how we deserve to be treated, respected, and listened to drives us to a prideful and arrogant position of boss. We must have the attitude of Jesus Christ.

> *"Therefore if you have any encouragement from being united with Christ, if any comfort from his love, if any common sharing in the Spirit, if any tenderness and compassion, 2 then make my joy complete by being like-minded,*

having the same love, being one in
spirit and of one mind. 3 Do nothing
out of selfish ambition or vain conceit.
Rather, in humility value others above
yourselves, 4 not looking to your own
interests but each of you to the
interests of the others."
Philippians 2:1-4

Paul further explains the humility of Jesus Christ and that our humility should be like his.

"In your relationships with one
another, have the same mindset as
Christ Jesus:6 Who, being in very
nature God, did not consider equality
with God something to be used to his
own advantage;7 rather, he made
himself nothing by taking the very
nature of a servant, being made in
human likeness. 8 And being found in
appearance as a man, he humbled
himself by becoming obedient to
death—even death on a cross!"
Philippians 2:5-8

Four areas that are needed to lead others well is to pray, think, love, and serve them as we train them up in the Lord.

Pray for them. Pray for their growth, understanding, personal needs, family, and for their heart to be continually filled with passion for Jesus. Pray for the people they lead. Pray for the mission God has given them. Pray for more faithful people for them to lead.

Think for them. Use your experience to be proactive instead of reactive. Think ahead of where they currently are. Try to prepare them for the things they will face instead of only dealing with the things they have already faced. Ask questions that lead them to the right answers or actions. Get them thinking. Train them to think proactively about their future.

Love them. Truly love them in a way that causes you to want their best everyday. Love is spelled "t-I-m-e." They don't care what you know until they know that you care. Spend time with them.

Serve them. Be a servant. Think of ways to serve them in their leadership. Try to take some of the things they are having to do off of them. Serve them in a way to ensure that they are successful.

Leadership is not as much about your success as it is about the success of the people who you are leading. You are a successful leader when the people you lead are successful.

MORE VERSES FOR STUDY AND REFLECTION

Galatians 6:9
I Timothy 4:12
Hebrews 13:17
Matthew 20:25-28
Jeremiah 3:15
Romans 12:9-10
Ephesians 4:11-16

CHAPTER 23

LIFE MANAGEMENT

You can plan your time, your day, and your life—or someone else will do it for you. How many of us have said, "Where has the time gone?" or "If I only had more hours in the day…?" We have the same number of hours in each day—most of us just don't use them well. We remain anxious about our week, every week. We sweat deadlines every time we are given one. We see our week as the thing that gets away from us every week.

Most people do not want to plan or organize their life because we feel we will then have a way to measure failure. When we finish the day and have things left on our to-do-today list that we were unable to accomplish, we feel a sense of inadequacy.

We think we are being more spiritual by just following the spirits leading throughout the day, and when He didn't lead, I just didn't do anything. The problem with this mindset is not in its leaning on the Holy Spirit's leading, because we do need to do this as will be discussed later in this chapter.

Rather, the problem is when we use the not-hearing-from-God-yet as an excuse to no activity at all. Also, before anyone throws the Mary and Martha story at me, I am not saying that we should be actively doing stuff while we should be being still and worshipping God. I am saying we should plan that into our life, as well. With no plan, we will quickly run out of time for everything, including that which is best. Most of us don't struggle with nothing to do.

We just struggle with which thing to do. Usually there is not simply good or bad that we must choose between. Often there is a bad, good, better, and a best. When we do not plan or organize our life, we take away the option to have the best we could have. We simply run out of time to discern and act.

"The plans of the heart belong to man, but the answer of the tongue is from the Lord. 2 All the ways of a man are pure in his own eyes, but the Lord weighs the spirit. 3 Commit your work to the Lord, and your plans will be established. 4 The Lord has made everything for its purpose, even the wicked for the day of trouble.
5 Everyone who is arrogant in heart is an abomination to the Lord; be assured, he will not go unpunished.
6 By steadfast love and faithfulness iniquity is atoned for, and by the fear of the Lord one turns away from evil.

7 When a man's ways please the Lord,he makes even his enemies to be at peace with him. 8 Better is a little with righteousness than great revenues with injustice. 9 The heart of man plans his way, but the Lord establishes his steps." Proverbs 16:1-9

We are encouraged to plan. We should plan, and we can have a plan. Our plan may not always match the Lord's steps, but He says that He will establish those for us.

"Trust in the Lord with all your heart, and do not lean on your own understanding. In all your ways acknowledge him, and he will make straight your paths."
Proverbs 3:5-6

"The wisdom of the prudent is to discern His ways."
Proverbs 14:8

"The plans of the diligent lead surely to abundance, but everyone who is hasty comes only to poverty."
Proverbs 21:5

God's word should be our guide as we plan, according to our heart. When our hearts are delighted in Him we make plans that bear His image. Basically, when we go to God in worship and prayer, he gives us our desires that match his desires. As we spend time with Him in His Word and in prayer, praise, and worship, we should then plan our life.

God is the owner of all. He has given us the role of managers. He is the owner, and we are the managers of our time, temple, talents and treasures. Time is the hours in each day, days in the week, weeks in the month, months in the year, years of life. He says that it is very short when compared with eternity. He says that our lives are but a vapor, here one moment and gone the next.

We need to be wise managers of the time He has given us. All the gifts He has given us are to be used for His Glory. Temple is the body with which God has blessed us, and we are the managers in how we take care of that which He has given us. We are responsible to take care of, nurture, and utilize our bodies for God's Glory.

Talents are those special areas that God has gifted us with in heart or abilities. Often, God uniquely blesses a group of believers with hearts or abilities for special areas of interests, and we are to plan to use those abilities and heart in those areas.

Treasures are those possessions with which God has blessed us to use for His glory. We need to also plan how to use that which he has given us as material possessions. Also, in this area we should be open to his leading and in determining the steps. Plan all of our life, organize all of our life, schedule all of our life—understanding that God may adjust the steps.

"For we are God's workmanship, created in Christ Jesus to do good works that he prepared in advance that we should walk in."
Ephesians 2:10

"in the story of the Good Samaritan, Jesus answers the question of what must we do to love our neighbor as ourselves by telling a story of a man. One man was traveling along the road from

*Jerusalem to Jericho and fell into the
hands of thieves. He was left beaten
and half naked on the side of the
road. One man, a Levite, came to the
man and crossed by on the other side
of the road. So also another man, a
priest, came to the man and crossed
by on the other side of the road. But a
Samaritan, as he traveled, came to
where the man was and took pity on
him, bandaged his wounds, and took
him to an inn where he paid the inn
keeper to care for him until he
returned. The Samaritan said that he
would repay the inn keeper for any
expenses. Jesus made his point very
clear by asking who was a neighbor to
the man who fell into the hands of the
thieves. Jesus then said, "Go, and do
likewise."*
Luke 10:25-37

I believe that this story also shows us
something very unique about the Samaritan. He did
not decide he would have a ministry to beaten,
robbed, half naked men on that road. No, it says as
he traveled, and this was not in his plan that day.
This was not on his to-do-today list. He planned his

course, and the Lord determined different steps. As he went on his planned way, the Lord determined steps that would require him to take pity on someone else.

The motivation to live this way comes from the fact that God has taken pity on us when we were not half dead, but dead in our sins and sinful nature. God made us alive in Christ! The fact that God did this very thing for us becomes the motivation for us to live our lives for a greater purpose than to please ourselves. Rather, He wants us to plan, organize, and lead our lives for His Glory, understanding full well that He may lead and empower us to different steps than we started with that day.

What was the motivation for the Samaritan to take pity on the man? Was it because he should "do onto others as he would have them do onto him?" Could it be that he was leaning on the leading of the Holy Spirit so well that God lead him to take pity? Was he specifically gifted in mercy, therefore, was he just exercising his gifts? All of these could be true.

The answer is not directly spoken about in the text. If we press in further, we can get more from the depths of the text. I believe that he took pity on the man who was half dead on the side of the road because he knew what it was like to be in that man's shoes.

*"And you were dead in the trespasses and sins **2** in which you once walked, following the course of this world, following the prince of the power of the air, the spirit that is now at work in the sons of disobedience— **3** among whom we all once lived in the passions of our flesh, carrying out the desires of the body and the mind, and were by nature children of wrath, like the rest of mankind. **4** But God, being rich in mercy, because of the great love with which he loved us, **5** even when we were dead in our trespasses, made us alive together with Christ—by grace you have been saved."*

Ephesians 2:1-5

He knew how awesome God is to have pity on us when we did not deserve it. Understanding the selfless love with which God has saved us motivated him to have the same love.

Plan, organize, and lead. But pray that you would be sensitive throughout your day to the leading of the Holy Spirit in you toward the things God desires of you each day. May he lead us all into the "good works that he prepared in advance that we should walk in."

> *"May our motivation to plan our lives for the Glory of God be the love of the Father for us."*
> *Ephesians 2:10*

Some very practical ways to manage your life is to have a plan. A plan consists of a few different quadrants; Urgent and important and all possibilities of them. There are four categories: Urgent and important, urgent and not important, important and not urgent, and not important and not urgent.

As your day, week, or month progresses, the things that need to be done change quadrants and are necessary to be on the to-do-today list. The items on the to-do-today list go on your daily schedule.

Realizing full well that as we plan, organize, and manage this life that God has given us, we must depend on the Holy Spirit's leading and empowering for the Jericho road steps to which He leads us.

URGENT AND IMPORTANT	URGENT AND NOT IMPORTANT
spend time with God take kids to school go to work finish report due today manage household budget	get additional phone charger for the house
IMPORTANT AND NOT URGENT next week's report kids have a school play next week to attend date night with my wife next Friday get oil changed, getting close to 3k miles get Christmas shopping done (it is Dec. 8)	**NOT IMPORTANT AND NOT URGENT** rake leaves redo mulch in flower beds

Many of the events we place on each quadrant can change as the activity becomes part of the current week. It may pass from not urgent to urgent.

Even raking the leaves may become urgent if your spouse is throwing a party that weekend and wants the yard to look nice. When the items become urgent then they move to the to-do list for the week.

Allow this tool to be what it is intended. Many people can simply make a master to-do list with everything on the list.

Others need the quadrants to make wise decisions about their schedule. For example, how many of us have cleaned our room or apartment before studying for a final?

Or cleaned our desk before writing a report with a deadline? Often we make those things to do that are less important or urgent first simply because it is easier to accomplish.

I also encourage all of us to spend time with God in His Word and prayer before planning the life He has allowed us to manage for His Glory.

"Your word is a lamp unto my feet and a light unto my path."
Psalm 119:105

Allow His Word, His Will, and His Spirit to guide you as you plan.

Next we take the Urgent/ Important quadrant and we place on the Master To-Do List for the week.

MONDAY	TUESDAY
plan for Wednesday night dinner	pick up kids from school
	make reservations for date-night dinner
discuss weekly goals with co-workers	staff meeting at work
buy light bulbs for outside entry lights	
begin grocery list	

WEDNESDAY	THURSDAY
take oldest child to orthodontist appointment	discuss braces with spouse for oldest child
confirm plans with everyone for dinner	begin week ending report
	plan for family time for the weekend
replace outside light bulbs	plan family meals for next week
drop off kids at youth group	finish grocery list
Wednesday night community group dinner	get groceries for next week

FRIDAY	SATURDAY/SUNDAY
finish week-ending report for work	get flowers for date night
go to accountability lunch	kids' sports events
finish last minute weekend planning	family time
	church
confirm with babysitter for Saturday night	planning time for next week
	rest

When we have a Master To-Do List it is easy to place each item on your Weekly or Daily Schedule. For some, a weekly glance schedule works best, for others a daily schedule is better.

	Mon	Tues	Wed	Thurs	Fri	Sat	Sun
6:00							
7:00							

	Mon	Tues	Wed	Thurs	Fri	Sat	Sun
8:00							
9:00							
10:00							
11:00							

While these tools allow for easier management of our daily lives, we must work at being disciplined to schedule time to plan. We must also be diligent to plan time to rest, to play, to pray, and to do all for which God has called us. We must be willing and ready to respond to His changing of our plans as we go.

The great commission for the church is found in **Matthew 28:19-20**.

"And Jesus came and said to them, "All authority in heaven and on

*earth has been given to me. 19 Go
therefore and make disciples of all
nations, baptizing them in the name of
the Father and of the Son and of the
Holy Spirit, 20 teaching them to
observe all that I have commanded
you. And behold, I am with you
always, to the end of the age."*
Matthew 28:19-20

In this verse the "Go" really implies "as you go." This means that we are seeking to fulfill the great commission as we go about our daily lives.

We all know that God has a plan for us. How could we think that he doesn't want us to plan this life He has given us to manage.

*"God has written a grand
narrative for each of us, and He is
committed to keeping us from writing
a lesser narrative than the one He has
already written."*
Bob Buford, Game Plan
(Buford, 1998)

MORE VERSES FOR FURTHER STUDY AND REFLECTION

Proverbs 21:5
Isaiah 32:8
Proverbs 3:5-6
Ephesians 5:15-17
Romans 12:1-2
I Corinthians 14:40
Matthew 6:25-34

CHAPTER 24

GOAL ACHIEVING

"God has written a grand narrative for you and is committed to keeping you from writing a lesser narrative than the one already written."

Bob Buford, Game Plan
(Buford, 1998)

A few years ago, a reporter was walking around Time Square in New York asking people about their New Year's resolutions. Each person stepped up to the microphone and answered in different ways, yet they all said about the same thing ... "I don't set any New Year's resolutions, because I never do any of them anyway."

This chapter is not about New Year's resolutions. However, this is a telling sign of what our culture has become. We don't set goals because we don't actually seek to achieve them.

In the last chapter, we discussed planning and organizing our lives. Hopefully we all learned how to utilize some great tools to maximize our effectiveness while also understanding that the Lord establishes the steps.

> *"The plans of the heart belong to man, but the answer of the tongue is from the Lord… In his heart man plans his course, but the Lord establishes his steps."*
> *Proverbs 16:1-9*

> *"I know the plans I have for you, declares the Lord, plans to prosper you, to give you hope and a future."*
> *Jeremiah 29:11*

Our hope is in our future deliverance from this world. Too often we read the verses that refer to our hope in Glory to our lives now. We easily put more emphasis on the present instead of the future.

Our culture tries to teach us Christians that this life is without trials if we are living it right. This couldn't be further from the truth. The trials are part of our training into maturity.

> *"Consider it pure joy, my brothers, whenever you face trials of many kinds, 3 because you know that the testing of your faith produces perseverance. 4 Let perseverance finish its work so that you may be mature and complete, not lacking anything."*
>
> James 1:2-4

Let's stop explaining away the sovereignty of our Lord in His establishing steps that are costly or uncomfortable in His maturing us as believers.

THE SECULAR/ SACRED DIVIDE

When we begin talking about our lives, goals, and things that we need to do, there is often a struggle to discern what is important. We can categorize our lives in such a way that certain things have greater importance.

This causes us to place greater emphasis on those things. For example, we Christians can place higher importance on the Spiritual things than on things we would call the mundane. We can say that the spiritual things are sacred and everything else is secular.

SACRED	SECULAR
Prayer, Bible study, church, house, taking kids to school,	Cleaning
fellowship, evangelism, kids plays, playing with the kids,	watching
missions, feeding the hungry, shopping, cooking, mowing the lawn	grocery
marriage counseling, etc. etc.	date night,

The divide between the sacred and the secular activities of our daily lives is not in what is being done, but rather who is doing it. When a Christian uses the lawn mower, he does so with a heart to please God. When a Christian cooks food, she does so with the desire to honor God. When a husband or wife is cleaning their home they work at it for the Glory of God.

"And whatever you do, whether in word or deed, do it all in the name of the Lord Jesus, giving thanks to God the Father through him."
Colossians 3:17

"So whether you eat or drink or whatever you do, do it all for the glory of God."
I Corinthians 10:31

So, when we wipe our babies' butts, we do it in the name of the Lord Jesus. When we clean the dishes, we do it for the glory of God. When we share the Gospel of Jesus Christ with our neighbor, we do it for God's glory.

There is no secular/ sacred divide for the Christian. God gets glory from every area of our lives, not because of our effort, but because He has redeemed us. Since He has redeemed us, and we are able to give all our effort in every area, knowing that because of Jesus, God is pleased with us.

GOAL ACHIEVING BEGINS WITH KNOWING OUR ROLES

Before we can set goals to achieve, we need to know the roles that God has given us. Knowing our roles will give us clarity on which areas require goals. Knowing the roles that He has given us provides clear tracks to run. If you are a mom, you can't question the role of being a mother.

Likewise, if you are a dad. If we understand the roles that God has given us, it streamlines the areas in which to set goals. We also can understand our weaknesses more obviously to plan, organize, and lead our lives for the Glory of God.

To be able to understand our roles we must take a step back and look at ourselves introspectively. We have to know ourselves and all that God has intended for us. For example, if you have children, then you know that you are entrusted to raise them in the way they should go. If God has granted you employment, then you understand there is a responsibility to provide for your family, etc.

Roles could fall in distinct categories, such as mother or father, son, Child of God, your career, homeowner, church member, etc. Roles can also fall into areas of gifting. For example, someone with the gift of mercy may have a specific way they serve their community, or someone with the gift of evangelism may have specific goals for sharing the Gospel.

We may also have roles that we play in others' lives. For example, we may be a little league coach, or volunteer for an organization. Understanding the roles that God has given you will help you to set only the goals in the areas for which you know He has placed you.

"Not that I have already obtained this or am already perfect, but I press on to make it my own, because Christ Jesus has made me his own. 13 Brothers, I do not consider that I have made it my own. But one thing I do: forgetting what lies behind and straining forward to what lies ahead, 14 I press on toward the goal for the prize of the upward call of God in Christ Jesus."

Philippians 3:12-14

"For we are God's workmanship, created in Christ Jesus, to do good works that he prepared in advance that we should walk in."

Ephesians 2:10

"Therefore, since we are surrounded by so great a cloud of witnesses, let us also lay aside every weight, and sin which clings so

closely, and let us run with endurance
the race that is set before us,"
Hebrews 12:1

Once we discern the roles that God has called us into we can know the areas in which to set goals. An additional helpful way to recall the goals of the roles is to write the motive or purpose statement of the goals next to each role. An example could be as follows:

- Father - I want to be the kind of father for my boys that I hope they will be for theirs.
- Husband - I want to love my wife in the depths of how she always dreamed she would be loved.
- Child of God - I want to exercise all that is mine in Christ Jesus in being God's adopted son.
- Employee - I want to work so diligently and thoughtfully as if my only boss was God himself.

These are examples of having very clear roles and motives of any goals that would come afterward.

Once we understand our roles, we can now learn how to set goals in each area.

Goals are simply maps of who we desire our future self to be—not simply things to accomplish. Those types of goals will come and go. When we set goals that change our lives, those are goals worth setting, therefore, they are worth pursuing. These are the goals that are similar to the goals that God has for us.

> *"And I am sure of this, that he who began a good work in you will bring it to completion at the day of Jesus Christ."*
> *Philippians 1:6*

His commitment is to continue to shape us into the image of Christ. We are His image bearers.

Our goals should be measurable, accountable, purposeful, and specific. These aren't just ideas. These are commitments to change who we are by specific attitudes and actions that we are willing to share and for which we should be accountable.

Measurable. This means that there is an easy way to measure the goal to be able to judge when this goal has been reached. An example is that

I want to treat the temple of God of my body with discipline to be more effective in energy and example for the next year.

The result of my goal is that I want to lose_____ inches around my waist, get nine hours of sleep per night, plan out my meals ahead of time, and exercise three times per week. The statistics make it measurable by goal and timing.

Accountable. This means that we are willing to be accountable to someone for the goal that we have set. This could be a workout partner at a gym, a financial advisor for our finances, a weekly accountability partner for Bible Study, a good friend about my marriage, my wife in how I lead my children, etc. An accountability partner is essential to help us stay the course in our goals.

"As Iron sharpens iron so one man sharpens another."
Proverbs 27:17

"Therefore, confess your sins to one another and pray for one another, that you may be healed. The prayer of a righteous person has great power as it is working."
James 5:16

Purposeful. This means that the goals serve a given purpose. This is the reason that the purpose statement beside each role is important. We generally do not pursue anything unless the purpose of that which we pursue is valid enough.

The goals must represent a greater purpose. I don't exercise my gift of hospitality for hospitality sake. I do it to meet the needs of people to share my greatest hope in life and death with them.

Specific. This means that we set these goals for our future with specified time lines. We can look forward and say that in the next five years I am going to be debt free. We then must make a plan that can help us to arrive at that specific goal.

That plan must have action steps throughout the five years—year 5, year 4, year 3, year 2, year 1, each month of year 1, this month, this week, today. If our goals are not specific enough in the plans we make to accomplish them, we will never get around to making the small decisions that will eventually help us to pursue these goals. Set the goals with the future in mind. Set the steps with the present at hand.

When we consider what God has given us to do and to be, we will take the purposes of our lives more seriously—serious enough to make MAPS of who we believe God wants us to become, share those Goals and surrender to accountability with someone who will commit with us to the changes necessary to 'do the good works that God has prepared in advance that we should walk in'. Ephesians 2:10

An example:

CHILD OF GOD - I want to exercise all that is mine in Christ Jesus in being God's adopted son.

1. I want to spend scheduled time alone with God in prayer and His Word on a daily basis.
2. I want to memorize one verse per week to place God's word in my heart as a lifetime habit.
3. I want to continue to remind myself of the truths from God about who he says I am.

FATHER - I want to be the kind of father for my boys that I hope they will be for theirs.

1. I want to pray with my boys every day and pray for them every night.
2. I want to teach my boys the truths of *The Bible* in every opportunity and twice per week.
3. I want to play with each boy concentrated time at least three hours per week.

HUSBAND - I want to love my wife in the depths of how she always dreamed she would be loved.

1. I want to have a date night with my wife that I plan twice per month.

2. I want to help my wife in cleaning and organizing the home on a weekly basis.
3. I want to pray for and with my wife everyday.

TEMPLE - I want to treat my body as the Temple of God and have more energy.

1. I want to exercise three days per week for at least 45 minutes of concentrated time.
2. I want to only eat until I am satisfied at meal times and regularly schedule my diet.
3. I want to rest each night for seven hours of sleep and have a full day of rest once per week.

EVANGELISM - I want to exercise my spiritual gift from God in a way that proclaims His name.

1. I want to continue to gain rapport with my neighbors, co-workers, and everywhere that I go
2. I want to move my relationships toward spiritual conversations that result in the Gospel.
3. I want to train men to be intentional in their relationships to be Gospel focused.

FINANCIAL MANAGER - I want to manage all that God has given me in a way that pleases Him.

1. I want to be debt free in five years of all debts (besides my house).
2. I want to pay all my bills on time.

3. I want to give more to my church, missionaries, and those around me who are in need.

> *"God has written a grand narrative for you and is committed to keeping you from writing a lesser narrative than the one already written."*
> *Bob Buford, Game Plan (Buford, 1998)*

MORE VERSES FOR FURTHER STUDY AND REFLECTION

Philippians 3:14
Hebrews 12:2
Proverbs 16:9
I Timothy 5:8
I Corinthians 9:24-27
Proverbs 21:5
James 4:13-15

CHAPTER 25

TALENTS

There is a popular performance-based, reality TV show called *America's Got Talent, Britain's Got Talent*, and so on. Everyone has talent. In this chapter, we are going to unwrap an acronym—TALENTS.

T- Temperament—This is the natural makeup of your personality.

A- Affections—These are the things about which you are passionate.

L- Life Experiences—This is the culmination of all major experiences in your life.

E- Education—This is the understanding you have to this point. It can be school or life education.

N- Need—This has two categories: What is the need in your life? What is the need around you?

T- Training—This is the depths of what you have been trained for or the training that you need.

S- Spiritual Gifts—These are the supernatural gifts that God has gifted you.

In order to understand your calling, your life, and lifestyle it would be helpful to have some deeper insight into how God has built you up to this point.

"O Lord, you have searched me and known me! You know when I sit down and when I rise up; you discern my thoughts from afar. You search out my path and my lying down and are acquainted with all my ways. Even before a word is on my tongue, behold, O Lord, you know it altogether. You hem me in, behind and before, and lay your hand upon me. Such knowledge is too wonderful for me; it is high; I cannot attain it. Where shall I go from your Spirit? Or where shall I flee from your presence? If I ascend to heaven, you are there! If I make my bed in Sheol, you are there! If I take the wings of the morning and dwell in the uttermost parts of the sea, even there your hand shall lead me, and your right hand shall hold me. If I say, "Surely the darkness shall cover me, and the light about me be night," even the darkness is not dark to you; the night is bright as the day, for darkness is as light with you. For you formed my inward parts; you knitted me together

*in my mother's womb. I praise you, for
I am fearfully and wonderfully made.
Wonderful are your works; my soul
knows it very well. My frame was not
hidden from you when I was being
made in secret, intricately woven in
the depths of the earth. Your eyes
saw my unformed substance; in your
book were written, every one of them,
the days that were formed for me,
when as yet there was none of them. "*
Psalm 132:1-16

He created and sustains everyone and everything. He knows you through and through. He has formed you, and He completes you.

*"And I am sure of this, that he
who began a good work in you will
bring it to completion at the day of
Jesus Christ."*
Philippians 1:6

He also works everything for our good and His Glory.

> *"And we know that for those who love God all things work together for good, for those who are called according to his purpose."*
> *Romans 8:28*

He also works things according to his purpose. To understand calling in our lives we must understand who He is and understand who we are. We are called according to his purpose—that is, according to his desires and design.

To better understand this we must have a shift in our focus. Too often our focus is on ourselves, our house, our money, our kids, our jobs, our rights, etc. We lose the exhortation from God to focus on Him.

> *"I appeal to you therefore, brothers, by the mercies of God, to present your bodies as a living sacrifice, holy and acceptable to God, which is your spiritual worship. Do not be conformed to this world, but be transformed by the renewal of your mind, that by testing you may discern what is the will of God, what is good and acceptable and perfect."*
> *Romans 12:1-2*

"Therefore, since we are surrounded by so great a cloud of witnesses, let us also lay aside every weight, and sin which clings so closely, and let us run with endurance the race that is set before us, looking to Jesus, the founder and perfecter of our faith, who for the joy that was set before him endured the cross, despising the shame, and is seated at the right hand of the throne of God. Consider him who endured from sinners such hostility against himself, so that you may not grow weary or fainthearted."

Hebrews 12:1-3

TEMPERAMENT

There are many different types of tests that help us to determine our temperament. They can be found online and only take 15 to 30 minutes to take and have your results. There are up to 16 different temperament categories. In one popular test, there are only four that fall into two categories of introvert and extravert. These are are dominant and influencing in the extravert, and steady and compliant in the introvert.

Those who have a Dominant temperament are direct, assertive, firm, and competitive. They tell rather than ask, make decisions on their own, move briskly, and speak rapidly. They are in command of the situation. The domineering type needs to ask people rather than tell them, let others help in decisions, and move slowly and more deliberately.

Those who have an Influencing temperament are persuasive and enthusiastic. They bring people along, move about freely, and are optimistically focused on the benefits of the situation. The influencing type needs to consider the facts before acting, take time to reflect, and set and maintain schedules.

Those who have a Steady temperament show support, are loyal, sympathetic, and patient. They have a need to be agreeable, respond to feelings, and care for the needs of others. The steady type needs to give in to always doing it their way. They need to take charge and learn how to say, "No."

Those who have a Compliant temperament are feel the need to be correct, literal, and complete. They emphasize standards, speak slowly and quietly, and report flaws or risk. The compliant type needs to be open to trying ideas without supportive data, increase volume and pace of speech, and be spontaneous at times while avoiding set plans.

Understanding your temperament can greatly assist you in understanding roles you should play on teams of people. Each temperament has very valuable strengths that generally are huge blind spots in the other temperaments.

But be aware that the negatives are as strong as the positives of each one. Knowing your natural personality tendencies can help you to depend on the Holy Spirit to open your mind and heart to how God wants you to respond in given circumstances rather than your normal reaction.

AFFECTIONS

Affections are those heartfelt leading toward passion for a cause, people group, need or activity. We all have specific passions excite us. We can have normal conversations about anything, but if this topic comes up we are going to talk five or ten times longer or more passionate about it. As we begin to think through the things for which we have a specific love, we are able to recognize a distinct gift of passion toward it that we carry with us.

Understanding our passion allows us to focus energy and effectiveness to cause change in the area toward which we have these affections. These passions can be the homeless, education, people from specific nationalities, dogs without homes, abortion, divorce, veterans, orphans, widows, individual rights or responsibilities, children, youth, college students, newly marrieds, senior citizens, needs of third-world countries, animals, etc.

We have these affections toward specific areas on purpose for a purpose. We should engage with like-minded people and research and study how we can act with a team in these areas.

LIFE EXPERIENCES

God is not just in control of the Cosmos. He is in control of the details of our lives. He didn't just create us, but he also sustains us in every way. He also created and sustains all of creation. He does not allow a single event to occur in our lives if he doesn't have a purpose for it.

We need to take some time to reflect on those benchmark life experiences to deduce all He has been doing in our lives to prepare us. All of them have purposes. We will never know all the ripple effects of the purposes of God through what He allows, but we can see some similarities and come to some clear understanding of his developing of our hearts and lives though our life experiences.

We should take a piece of paper and write 3-10 years, 11-15 years, 16-18 years, 19-22 years, 23-29 years, 30-35 years, 36-40 years, 41-45 years, 46-50 years, and so forth. After you have these columns written across a page, begin to write significant events that occurred in your life during those years.

Look for patterns, ideas that repeated, significant achievements, any lifestyle changes that were important, family life changes, job or living arrangement changes. Begin to look for God at work in every area throughout your life to attempt to see what He was doing and for what he was preparing you. Marvel at His faithfulness, smile with anticipation, mourn the sorrows, but realize that He knew what He was doing and allowing even when we didn't.

He began a good work in your life at salvation, and He is committed to continuing the work in your life to completion. ee what He has been doing. Join Him.

EDUCATION

We all have an education. Some have received their education from prominent schools with decorated degrees. Some have Magna Cum Laude said after their name as they walk across the stage to receive their diploma. Others have an education from the school of life. We all have an education, but what have we really learned? Some are able to read and learn. It's that simple.

Others have to go through the circumstance to learn. A friend says that some learn while others have to earn their education. His meaning is that we have to go through the situation before we have learned the lesson.

What is your education? What have you learned? How do you apply what you have learned to your life? Are there people who have played a large role in your education? Have you learned without passing what you have learned on to others? Who will put your name down as the one who played a large role in their life?

When we discern God's will for our life through the temperament, affections, and life experiences He gave us. we can begin to understand why. Yes, Why? God, Why did you do this? Why have you made me like this?

We will eventually come to the amazing conclusion that God creates and sustains us on purpose and for a purpose. The Westminster Catechism says in the opening question, "What is the chief end of man?" This question is asking why does mankind exist.

The answer is, "To Glorify God and enjoy Him forever." He designed us and sustains us for His

Glory and our enjoyment of Him. He made us on purpose and for a purpose. What is yours?

NEED

What is the need around you? What is the need in your life for which you should act? What is your immediate need? What is your family's need?

As you discover your design by God, you will begin to notice some new and improved focus on your passions. This generally will create some action, or at least a call to action. Once He begins illuminating your mind with His will, there will be some needs.

> *"And my God can supply all your needs according to His Glorious riches in Christ Jesus."*
> *Philippians 4:19*

This verse is referring to needs being met by God, not every whim and want.

Another question is to ask yourself is if the things that God is showing you are needs around you. Does your area need this?

Another question to ask yourself is while observing all that God has done in you and through you up to this point is there a need in you to pass these passions on. I need to do _____.

A final question to ask yourself is if God is truly leading you to act on your passions and His vision for you. Is there an immediate need for you to do? For example, should you get a new job, (don't quit your current job until you have a new one), be present more for your family, lead your wife better, give your husband a chance to lead in the family, pay bills, lead those around you, etc.? Is there a need today as you prepare to act on the next step?

TRAINING

While temperaments, affections, life experience, education, and need are all important, training is of utmost importance. We all need training in many areas of our lives. In what areas do you need training? In what ways can you get the training that you need? Who can train you?

We can have all the education in the world, however, without the training to apply it, it isn't very useful. Training sets the temperament, affections, life experience, education and need to work. Training gifts all the ideas tracks to run on.

We can find a mentor somewhere who has been doing that which I believe God is leading me to do. How am I going to get time to be trained? Who is going to train me? When? Where?

As we answer these questions we can begin to get excited about the path that God has us on with all new vigor.

> *"To this end I labor, working*
> *with all His energy which so*
> *powerfully works in me."*
> Colossians1:2<u>9</u>

SPIRITUAL GIFTS

I believe that all the things we have discussed are gifts from God. Spiritual gifts are the next level. These are not the ones we have been discussing which are natural. These are supernatural. The spiritual gifts are specific gifts that God has given to His children for the direct purpose to Glorify Him and enjoy him forever and to bless others.

There are many spiritual gifts tests that you can take and see the results in 15-30 minutes. These online tests also have printable material that can explain the details of the gifts. Understanding these specific gifts from God in your arsenal are valuable and worth the time to know how He has gifted you and how those gifts can be used for His Glory.

Here is a list of spiritual gifts from *The Bible* in Romans 12, I Corinthians 12 and Ephesians 4:

Administration	Knowledge
Apostleship	Leadership
Discernment	Mercy
Evangelism	Miracles
Exhortation	Pastor/Shepherd
Faith	Prophecy
Giving	Healing
Teaching	Tongues
Wisdom	Serving/Ministering

Others found in *The Bible* are: celibacy, hospitality, martyrdom, missionary, voluntary, and poverty.

> *"God has written a grand narrative for you, and is committed to keeping you from writing a lesser narrative than the on already written."*
> *Bob Buford, Game Plan*
> *(Buford, 1998)*

"I appeal to you therefore, brothers, by the mercies of God, to present your bodies as a living sacrifice, holy and acceptable to God, which is your spiritual worship. Do not be conformed to this world, but be transformed by the renewal of your mind, that by testing you may discern what is the will of God, what is good and acceptable and perfect."
Romans 12:1-2

Eric Liddel was an Olympic athlete from Scotland who was considered to be the fastest man on the planet. He was an Olympic Gold medalist runner, and he was a believer. He used his talent as a runner to share the Gospel of Jesus Christ with everyone. His whole family were missionaries to China.

In a movie depicting his life and faith called *Chariots of Fire*, his sister confronts him about going to China as a missionary. He responded, "I know that God made me for a purpose, but He also made me fast. And when I run, I feel His pleasure."

Find how God has made you, and then discover what you do that while you do it you feel His pleasure. Afterward, develop your TALENTS to the fullest.

"The thief comes to steal, kill and destroy; but I have come that you may have life and life to the fullest."
John 10:10

MORE VERSES FOR FURTHER STUDY AND REFLECTION

Ephesians 4:11-16
Psalm 139:13-16
Ephesians 2:10
Jeremiah 29:11
Psalm 139:1-5
John 15:16
II Corinthians 5:17-20

CHAPTER 26

VALUES-VISION-RESOLUTIONS

VALUES

> *In ethics, value denotes something's degree of importance, with the aim of determining what action of life is best to do or live. Values can be defined as broad preferences concerning appropriate courses of action or outcomes. As such, values reflect a person's sense of right and wrong or what "ought" to be.*
> *Wikipedia definition of values.*

Values are those ideals that define who we are, and also refine in us who we desire to be. We constantly hear about behavior that is questionable, and we say, "Well, they just have no values."

Values are not just good ideas that you hold, rather they are ideals that hold you. We may prescribe to certain ideals in our lives, yet if what we do and who we are do not reflect those ideals, then these are not yet our values.

If we do not clearly set those things that we value in our life, others will. We cannot wait until the culture moves what is acceptable so far from what we hold important. We must not allow our culture to make the decisions that determine the content of our character.

Values are often listed on the wall of most businesses; "We value great food and great service." or "We fix it right the first time." or "We handle your business as if it were our business." Many businesses have little catchy phrases in an attempt to single them out as the best in one category or another. They are sharing the things that they value to express what you will get if you do business with them. Their values express what you can expect from them and their employees.

Our values should do the same. What we value should be evident in our life. People should meet us, get to know us and be able to see our values.

Categories that we have values in may include: family, work, finance, relationships, communication, rights, responsibilities, etc.

"If we stand for nothing we will fall for anything." Having a list of values in our lives ensures that we know what we stand for.

We can guess which values are important, or we can just let our culture tell us, or we can be proactive in our search for what should have value in our lives. Instead of running to the headlines or the TV commercials or news of what is going on in our culture, lets run to the Word of God to find what He holds to great value.

When we find the values of our lives in the scriptures, we can rest in that we are basing our values on truth. We can also rest in the fact that God is committed to empowering us to pursue these values with His power that is at work within us.

> *"To this end I labor with His energy that so powerfully works in me."*
> *Colossians 1:29*

> *"for it is God who works in you, both to will and to work for his good pleasure."*
> *Philippians 2:13*

"For you are God's workmanship, created in Christ Jesus to do good works that he prepared in advance for you to walk in."
Ephesians 2:10

VISION

Vision and Mission are often linked together as the same thing. However, mission should be the response to vision. For example, we do not understand what the mission needs to accomplish if we do not know the needs around us. Vision is the seeing of what is truly going on around us and having the capacity to understand the needs that exist.

Too often we are so focused on our little bubble that we never recognize what is going on outside of our immediate concerns. The biggest issue is that the immediate concerns are most likely only the concerns of our own well being. Most of us live for our own good or profit. We live for the now and for the now for us alone for the most part.

To see that which is going on around us requires some degree of thinking of yourself less. This is the definition of humility. Humility is not thinking less of yourself, rather it is the discipline of considering others' needs above your own.

> "Do nothing from selfish ambition or conceit, but in humility count others more significant than yourselves. *4* Let each of you look not only to his own interests, but also to the interests of others. *5* Have this mind among yourselves, which is yours in Christ Jesus, *6* who, though he was in the form of God, did not count equality with God a thing to be grasped, *7* but emptied himself, by taking the form of a servant, being born in the likeness of men. *8* And being found in human form, he humbled himself by becoming obedient to the point of death, even death on a cross."
> Philippians 2:3-8

Most of our problem of not seeing clearly what is going on around us is due to the fact that we like to focus on ourselves. Walk into any bookstore, and the largest section will be the "self- help" books.

Midlife crisis used to mean you traded in your economy car for a convertible sports car.

The new midlife crisis is to reinvent yourself through going to the gym, trading in your committed relationship with your spouse for a newer, younger one, or altering your style to whatever the magazines determine is up to date. We are in a crisis, alright! It is a crisis of not seeing clearly the world in which we live. We have dumbed down relationships to be whichever form of social media we use as the main method of communication, rather than looking people in the eyes, shaking hands firmly, and being in their actual physical presence.

We see what is going on in the world through scrolling our Facebook news feed instead of looking at the people around us. We communicate better through social media with people halfway across the world instead of in person with our next-door neighbor or co-workers. We need new vision for the world in which we live.

> *"The most pathetic person in the world is someone who has sight, but has no vision."*
> *Helen Keller*

Go to the website: www.worldometers.info (World O Meters, n.d.) and prepare to be shocked. I am looking at this information on February 9, 2016 at 10:30 am.

- Current population of the world is more than 7.4 billion.
- Deaths already today is 72,000.
- Public Healthcare is $4.85 billion spent today.
- Public Education is $4.26 billion spent today.
- Money spent on video games today is $87.6 million.
- There are currently 3.3 billion Internet users, which accounts for 44.5% of the world population.
- There are 778.6 million undernourished people with 1.6 billion overweight people, with over 13,500 people who died of hunger so far today in the world.
- There has been $218.5 million spent on obesity-related disease with $83.9 million on weight-loss programs in the United States today.
- There have been more than 194,000 deaths related to water this year in the world.
- There are 666.7 million people with no access to safe drinking water in the world today, while the world is using more than 1,169,638,000 million liters of water this year.

- Around the world, $43 billion has been spent on illegal drugs this year.
- Smoking caused 540,000 deaths this year with 6.7 billion cigarettes smoked this year.
- Also, there have been 4.5 million deaths by abortion this year.

IT'S FEBRUARY 9 at 10:30 a.m.! Let's wake up from our slumber and realize that this world is sick! It has only been 16 minutes since I wrote the amount of money spent on obesity in the U.S. and it has already increased by $4 million. Money spent on video games has already increased another $2.6 million. **What is going on in this world?**

> *"The Lord saw that the wickedness of man was great in the earth, and that every intention of the thoughts of his heart was only evil continually. 6 And the Lord regretted that he had made man on the earth, and it grieved him to his heart."*
> *Genesis 6:5*

There is a great sickness that has spread throughout the world in which we live. It has caused more decay than the diseases, cancers, and even hunger. It has brought the results mentioned above.

The cause of the decay of our world can be classified across the board as SIN. We can cast blame in all kinds of directions. We can blame governments, agencies for world hunger relief, politicians, kings, etc.

The truth is we love ourselves more than our neighbor, more than the needy, more than the hungry, more than those dying of thirst, literally. There is enough money, enough people, enough energy, enough resources, enough of everything in the world to solve the problems of the world. We do have a problem—a major problem in this world. Sin has plagued our hearts to desire good for ourselves even at the cost of others. Until our hearts have been transformed we will not make advances toward the real problems of this world.

"And I will give you a new heart, and a new spirit I will put within you. And I will remove the heart of stone from your flesh and give you a heart of flesh."
Ezekial 36:26

This process of transforming the heart is called regeneration. Regeneration is a process of God changing the heart of man, by the power of the Holy Spirit, through the person and work of Jesus Christ living the perfect life and dying the sinner's death on the cross for us.

Until God has regenerated our hearts we do not truly have a heart for mankind that is necessary to love our neighbor, countrymen, people from other countries in a way that can bring about real change. Until our hearts have been changed by God, we will not do what is necessary.

> *"So if there is any encouragement in Christ, any comfort from love, any participation in the Spirit, any affection and sympathy, 2 complete my joy by being of the same mind, having the same love, being in full accord and of one mind. 3 Do nothing from selfish ambition or conceit, but in humility count others more significant than yourselves. 4 Let each of you look not only to his own interests, but also to the interests of others. 5 Have this mind among yourselves, which is yours in Christ*

Jesus, 6 who, though he was in the form of God, did not count equality with God a thing to be grasped, 7 but emptied himself, by taking the form of servant, being born in the likeness of men. 8 And being found in human form, he humbled himself by becoming obedient to the point of death, even death on a cross."
Philippians 2:1-8

We must confess our selfishness and seek God's forgiveness. We may then look beyond ourselves to the needs of those around us. We may humbly serve our neighbor, co-workers, homeless, helpless, hungry etc.

"It is forgiveness that sets a man working for God. He does not work in order to be forgiven, but because he has been forgiven, and the consciousness of his sin being pardoned makes him long for its entire removal than ever he did before. An unforgiven man cannot work. He has not the will, nor the power, nor the liberty. He is in chains.

*Israel in Egypt could not serve
Jehovah. "Let my people go, that they
may serve Me." was God's message
to Pharaoh (exodus 8:1) first liberty,
then service. A forgiven man is the
true worker, the true law-keeper. He
can, he will, he must work for God. He
has come into contact with that part of
God's character which warms his cold
heart. Forgiving love constrains him.
He cannot but work for Him who has
removed his sins from him as far as
the east is from the west. Forgiveness
has made him a free man, and given
him a new and most loving master.
Forgiveness, received freely from the
God and Father of our Lord Jesus
Christ, acts as a spring, an impulse, a
stimulus of divine potency. It is more
irresistible than law, or terror, or
threat."*

Horatius Bonar (Bonar, 2012)

What should we do? What can we do? How
can we do it? When do we start?

We can no longer sit on the sidelines and only
hope something happens. We must engage the

culture. We must act. We must join the game instead of simply spectating.

> *"So whoever knows the right thing to do and fails to do it, for him it is sin."*
> *James 4:17*

We must see locally what is going on and pray for God to give us clear vision of what He desires of us to do, then by the power of the Holy Spirit, get to work!

> *"The only way the corporate Body of Christ will fulfill the mission Christ has given it is for individual Christians to have a vision for fulfilling that mission personally."*
> *David Jeremiah, Compelled (Rutherford, 2018)*

RESOLUTIONS

Resolutions are usually viewed as those statements that we make at each New Year that will surely fall away a few weeks later and then be remembered again at the end of that year that was supposed to be spent achieving that resolution.

We need to reclaim the word to resolve to do something or to be someone. We have made it into an odd annual ritual. Let's take it much deeper than that. May we look into the depths of our soul to find those things that we believe that God desires of us.

Let's confess those things in a way that continually reminds us of Him and his commitment to us. May our motivation be in light of what God has done for us in His commitment to us who do not deserve it. Perhaps we can express our commitment to Him who does deserve it.

"Jonathan Edwards, 1703-58, American theologian and metaphysician, was born in East Windsor. He was a precocious child, early interested in things scientific, intellectual, and spiritual. After graduating from Yale at 17, he studied theology, preached (1722-23) in New York City, tutored (1724-26) at Yale, and in 1727 became the colleague of his grandfather, Solomon Stoddard, in the ministry at Northampton, Mass. In 1729, on his grandfather's death,

> *Edwards took sole charge of the congregation. The young minister was not long in gaining a wide following by his forceful preaching and powerful logic."*
>
> *Society of Colonial Wars in the State of Connecticut website (Society of Colonial Wars in the State of Connecticut, n.d.)*

His preaching was influential in the first Great Awakening specifically in New England.

Jonathan Edwards wrote the first 21 resolutions that would ultimately guide his life and faith in 1722, he finished the rest of the 70 resolutions in August of 1723. He was very clearly a principled man, who understood the value of not simply believing, but confessing what he believed and desired to live out in his daily life.

> *"Being sensible that I am unable to do anything without God's help, I do humbly entreat him by his grace to enable me to keep these resolutions, so far as they are agreeable to his will, for Christ's sake."*

*Introduction to the 70
resolutions by Jonathan Edwards
(Edwards, 2001)*

After this statement he simply wrote, "Remember to read over these resolutions once a week." Here are a few samples of his resolutions:

13.   "Resolved, that I will live so as I shall wish I had done when I come to die."

24.   "Resolved, whenever I do any conspicuously evil action, to trace it back, till I come to the original cause; and then both carefully endeavor to do so no more, and to fight and pray with all my might against the original of it."

28.   "Resolved, to study the Scriptures so steadily, constantly and frequently, as that I may find, and plainly perceive myself to grow in the knowledge of the same."

41.   "Resolved, to ask myself at the end of every day, week, month and year, wherein I could possibly in any respect have done better."

Take the time to sit, pray and listen to the Holy Spirit lead you to that which He desires you to be resolved to be and do.

MORE VERSES FOR FURTHER STUDY AND REFLECTION

Hebrews 10:23
I Thessalonians 2:12
II Peter 1:3
Philippians 1:6
Proverbs 3:5-6
Isaiah 40:31
Jeremiah 29:11

CHAPTER 27

LIFE MISSION

What is the chief end of man? To glorify God and enjoy Him Forever. [Westminster Confession of Faith and Catechisms as adopted by the Presbyterian Church of America by the Orthodox Presbyterian Church (Church, 2007)]

In asking this question, we are unpacking more questions, including, "Why are we here? Why do we exist? Why did God make us?"

After reading the book, *Desiring God by John Piper* (Piper, 1986), I was deeply challenged in my thinking about God's glory and my happiness. I had always struggled with the idea that these two focuses somehow contradicted one another.

I learned that God's Glory has a lot in common with my joy. He designed us. He planned our lives. He is sovereign in his control and leadership of our lives. He knows our desires and knows best how to meet all the needs of our hearts. He can do all of this while empowering us to enjoy Him while He glorifies Himself through our lives.

"O Lord, you have searched me and known me! 2 You know when I sit down and when I rise up; you discern my thoughts from afar. 3 You search out my path and my lying down and are acquainted with all my ways. 4 Even before a word is on my tongue, behold, O Lord, you know it altogether. 5 You hem me in, behind and before, and lay your hand upon me. 6 Such knowledge is too wonderful for me; it is high; I cannot attain it. you formed my inward parts; you knitted me together in my mother's womb. . .14 I praise you, for I am fearfully and wonderfully made. Wonderful are your works; my soul knows it very well. 15 My frame was not hidden from you, when I was being made in secret, intricately woven in the depths of the earth.16 Your eyes saw my unformed substance; in your book were written, every one of them, the days that were formed for me, when as yet there was none of them.'

Psalm 139:1-6 and 14-16

*"Delight yourself in the LORD,
and he will give you the desires of
your heart."*
Psalm 37:4

*"God is most glorified in us,
when we are most satisfied in Him."*
*[Desiring God by John Piper
(Piper, 1986)]*

Too often we believe that the obedient Christian life can only be obtained by our sacrifice of all our wants, desires, and joys. This can be true if all of our wants, desires, and joys are centered around sin.

However, if our wants, desires, and joys are centered around our relationship with God, then there is no need to sacrifice our joy for His glory. Our joy will become His glory if we delight in Him.

As you begin to try to unpack the answer to the question, "What is my Life Mission?" we must look inside our hearts to discern our passions and desires from a Christ-centered perspective. We must look at our lives through the lenses of God's view. How can I live in light of God's calling? How has God gifted me? How has God designed me? What does He want from me?

> *"For we are God's workmanship, created in Christ Jesus for good works that he prepared in advance that we should walk in."*
> *Ephesians 2:10*

Not only has God designed us, but He has also prepared for us an amazing life. This life He has for us is full and abundant.

> *"...He came that we might have life and to the fullest." John 10:10*
> *"Therefore, I urge you, brothers and sisters, in view of God's mercy, to offer your bodies as a living sacrifice, holy and pleasing to God--this is your spiritual act of worship. Do not conform any longer to the pattern of this world, but be transformed by the renewing of your mind. Then you will be able to test and approve what*

God's will is--his good, pleasing and
perfect will."
Romans 12:1-2

This verse is very clear about how to discover God's will for your life. It begins in verse 1 by urging us, in view of God's mercy. We must look into the mercies of God as we attempt to discover His will for our lives. His mercy is Him not giving us what we deserve. We deserve to pay for the debt of our sins to God through an eternity in Hell.

However, God's mercy has delivered us from the penalty of our sin into the acceptance into adoption by God as sons and daughters. *The Bible* is clear that His mercies are new every morning (Lamentations 3:22-23).

Viewing his mercy for us in sending his Son, Jesus Christ, to die in our place acts as a catalyst for increasing our desire to offer ourselves unto Him as a living sacrifice. This living sacrifice is holy and pleasing to God because Jesus has made us holy. The verse says to no longer conform our lives to the patterns of this world, but to be transformed by the renewing of our mind.

Our mind is renewed as we run to God in repentance, turning from our sin unto God. He forgives our sins and cleanses us from all unrighteousness (I John 1:9). We then invest time in

His word to discover that which He desires of us. As we cling to His mercy, repent of our sin, and study his word, He reveals his good, pleasing, and perfect will for our lives.

> *"God has written a grand narrative for each of us, and is committed to keeping us from writing a lesser narrative than the one he's already written."*
> Bob Buford, Game Plan.

God desires to reveal his plans to us as we are ready for them.

> *"Your word is a lamp unto my feet and a light unto my path."*
> Psalm 119:105

This verse clearly explains that God's word is a step-by-step guide for us according to His will and desire for us.

The greatest commandment found in *The Bible* is in Luke 10:27.

> *"And he answered, "You shall love the Lord your God with all your*

heart and with all your soul and with
all your strength and with all your
mind, and your neighbor as yourself."
Luke 10:27

In explaining how we should love God, it explains that we should love God with all our emotion and passion, with all our being, with all our energies, and with all of our thoughts. This verse also says that we should love our neighbor as we love ourselves. The rest of the chapter explains who we should treat as a neighbor, and it includes everyone, from everywhere, as we go, wherever we go.

For what were you designed?

What makes you feel passionate?

How do you sense God leading you?

As you dive into His word and trust in Him, he will begin to unwrap direction for your life.

Pray, seek his face, seek his word, and seek counsel from those around you who know you well. This will help you discern his good, pleasing, and perfect will for your life.

Do not be discouraged if He only reveals small steps in the beginning as you seek Him. Remember that He is perfectly sovereign over all, and His timing is perfect, as well.

CALLING

When it comes to our calling, we often falsely believe that God's call is only extended to people to go into full-time vocational ministry. God does call people in this way. However, He also calls people into all different types of vocations for ministry. God has a great vision of using us in every field, every career, every relationship, every sphere of influence that He gives us.

God's calling aligns with His design of our gifts. He prepares the good works that he planned in advance for us, and He also prepares us for those good works. (Ephesians 2:10)

At the 1924 Summer Olympics in Paris, Eric Liddell refused to run in the heats for his favored 100-meter event because they were scheduled on a Sunday. He instead competed in the 400-meter event, in which he won the gold medal.

In the movie that depicts his story, *Chariots of Fire*, his sister asks him to go to China as a missionary with the rest of his family.

He responds, *"I know God made me for a purpose, but he also made me fast; and when I run I feel his pleasure."* After his racing career was finished, Eric did join his family in China as a Christian missionary. However, he was a Christian missionary already as a highly popular, well-known athlete.

William Wilberforce is another example of a man who had a struggle with his calling as he was trying to discern God's call on his life. He was born into nobility in British parliament, yet he had become a new believer in Christ.

He thought very deeply about the potential call of God on his life into full-time vocational ministry. Some other Godly men approached him about the slave-trade problems and told him that they believed that he could have a much larger impact on the world by remaining in Parliament as a believer and serving the cause of abolishing the slave trade.

William Wilberforce entered Parliament in 1784. In 1785, he became a Christian. In 1787, he was approached to fight to abolish the slave trade for which he fought for more than 20 years until finally the passage of The Slave Trade Act of 1807.

We do not know the future, nor do we automatically understand how God has gifted us, or called us to act on His behalf toward His creation for His Glory. However, we can look at our lives and see what we do that makes us "feel" his pleasure. We can look to those around us to help us discern that for which God has designed us. We can follow God closely, day after day, trusting Him for the next step in discovering our calling.

MORE VERSES FOR FURTHER STUDY AND REFLECTION

II Timothy 4:6-8
Hebrews 12:1-3
Matthew 9:37-38
Psalm 37:4
Colossians 3:17
Colossians 1:28-29
Matthew 28:18-20

CHAPTER 28

TEAM

Understanding that God designed us for community is essential to understanding the body of Christ. He chose for Himself a people, not simply a person. He bought us together to be interdependent. The idea of co-dependency communicates that we are dependent on one another only, however interdependence is the idea that we are together depending on God.

We are in this together. His design for us is to work together, live in community with one another, achieve good works that he planned in advance for us together. He also has gifted us accordingly. He has given gifts to the body of Christ to work efficiently together in the areas that He has gifted each one.

As we work together according to our gifting, we are able to focus more on the areas for which we are equipped as well as the areas that we enjoy doing more. Less time spent on the things that we are not gifted to do maintains more focus and energy than doing the things we are gifted to do.

When we have a group of believers who are utilizing their gifting to the fullest it permits us to operate within our gifting, as well. We become a well-oiled machine with each part doing its work.

*"For the body does not consist of one member but of many. **15** If the foot should say, "Because I am not a hand, I do not belong to the body," that would not make it any less a part of the body. **16** And if the ear should say, "Because I am not an eye, I do not belong to the body," that would not make it any less a part of the body. **17** If the whole body were an eye, where would be the sense of hearing? If the whole body were an ear, where would be the sense of smell? **18** But as it is, God arranged the members in the body, each one of them, as he chose. **19** If all were a single member, where would the body be? **20** As it is, there are many parts, yet one body. **21** The eye cannot say to the hand, "I have no need of you," nor again the head to the feet, "I have no need of you." **22** On the contrary, the parts of the body that seem to be weaker are indispensable, **23** and on those parts of the body that we think less honorable we bestow the greater honor, and our unpresentable parts*

are treated with greater modesty,
***24** which our more presentable parts do not require. But God has so composed the body, giving greater honor to the part that lacked it, **25** that there may be no division in the body, but that the members may have the same care for one another. **26** If one member suffers, all suffer together; if one member is honored, all rejoice together."*

I Corinthians 12:14-26

*"And he gave the apostles, the prophets, the evangelists, the shepherds and teachers, **12** to equip the saints for the work of ministry, for building up the body of Christ, **13** until we all attain to the unity of the faith and of the knowledge of the Son of God, to mature manhood, to the measure of the stature of the fullness of Christ, **14** so that we may no longer be children, tossed to and fro by the waves and carried about by every wind of doctrine, by human cunning,*

by craftiness in deceitful schemes.
15 *Rather, speaking the truth in love,*
we are to grow up in every way into
him who is the head, into Christ,
16 *from whom the whole body, joined*
and held together by every joint with
which it is equipped, when each part
is working properly, makes the body
grow so that it builds itself up in love."
Ephesians 4:11-16

In studying TEAM, the idea of who you want to work with to accomplish the mission that God has led you to comes into play. We must know the needs around us to discern the mission that God has given us. We must also know how we are gifted to know the role we must play in the mission. We then need to assemble the right TEAM with the gifts necessary to accomplish the mission.

TEAM BUILDING

In building a team of people there are a few things that must be considered—character, calling, and chemistry. The goal of any team is to be sure that all members of the team are united with a similar mission. The next stage is to determine the character of those you would want on your team or the team with which you would want to be involved. An additional step is to be sure that the calling is to the well-defined mission. Lastly, the way that the members get along, fit together, and are able to work together determine the correct chemistry among the team.

After building a team of people to accomplish a given mission, we must be sure that each member of the team has distinct responsibilities that align with their temperament and gifts. The imagery of an airplane can be used for this. We must make sure that the right people are on the plane, and that they are all in the correct seat. The seats represent the different roles. For example, the flight attendant does not need to be in the pilot's seat and vice versa. Also, the most nervous passenger does not need to be in the exit row. We must be sure our team is in the correct role.

CHURCH/ NONPROFIT/ COLLECTIVE/ PARTNERING/ MERGING

As we look to meet the needs in the areas around us with great vision we must set forth a very clear mission according to our calling and with a team. For some of us, we can have our local body of believers, our church, as our team. For some other more specific ministries, we may need to establish a separate ministry or nonprofit that directly affects a given need.

Some needs can utilize both with a nonprofit organization that can attract many other already established churches, businesses, or individuals to team with to accomplish the given mission. This collaboration of churches, businesses, or organizations is called a collective. Depending on the size of the mission, one may need to look at a collective of groups or teams to collaborate with in order to be able to accomplish the mission.

There can be many different methods of teaming together, there are partnerships where different groups may collaborate on a few different projects that promote both interests. There are mergers where two entities combine into one team working with the common mission.

Another method of developing a team around a mission is to investigate to see if there is anyone else doing something similar in your area or others that you can glean some strategies or systems from to be able to implement in your area. Even if the other group is not close enough to partner or merge with, there is plenty of education and methods of implementation that may work not dependent on the culture of where it is happening.

Many churches are now working outside the box in the areas of ministry on which they are focusing. In the facilities, they are meeting more needs in the communities where they live and to love the cities well in how they exist. Some churches are opening businesses as a place of worship on Sundays and making it an inviting atmosphere throughout the week to meet the needs of people in their community. This meeting place can help to build relationships in a laid-back setting.

Other churches are utilizing some great needs in their city to develop a ministry hub that also doubles as a worship center. Some are meeting in gymnasiums, schools, store fronts, businesses, etc. The context of ministry is rapidly adjusting to the culture in which it is called to impact, while recognizing that without contact there is no impact.

The churches that are really making a difference in seeing hearts transformed by the Grace of God have learned to alter their context without altering the content of historically accurate Biblical orthodoxy.

This is an effective option to building expensive buildings and calling them a "church" and telling the culture, "please come." The church is going to the people and telling them about the love of God. This method of going into the culture is literally the same way that God did it by sending His son, Jesus Christ, into the world to live in it among the people of His time and to impact them by proclaiming the love of God. Our calling is not so different.

How will we live among the people of our time and impact them?

With whom will we do this?

How will we define our roles?

When will we do this?

MORE VERSES FOR FURTHER STUDY AND REFLECTION

I Corinthians 12:20-25

Romans 12:4-5

III John 1:8

Proverbs 11:14

I Corinthians 1:10

Philippians 2:1-5

Ecclesiastes 4:9-12

WORKS CITED

(n.d.). Retrieved from World O Meters: www.worldometers.info

Bonar, H. (2012). *God's Way of Holiness.* CreateSpace Independent Publishing Platform.

Bounds, E. (1990). *The Complete Works of E.M. Bounds on Prayer.* Baker Books.

Buford, B. P. (1998). *Game Plan.* Grand Rapids, MI: Zondervan.

Calvin, J. (2009). *Calvin's Commentaries.* Baker Books.

Chandler, M. (n.d.). *The Explicit Gospel.* Crossway.

Church, T. O. (2007). *Westminster Confession of Faith and Catechisms as Adopted by the Presbyterian Church in America.* Christian Education & Publications.

Coleman, R. E. (2010). *The Master Plan of Evangelism.* Revell.

Comfort, R. (2011). *The Evidence Bible.* Bridge-Logos Publishers.

Edwards, J. (2001). *Jonathan Edwards Resolutions and Advise to Young Converts .* P & R Publishing.

Fisher, T. (2017). *A Few Buttons Missing.* Muriwai Books.

Foster, R. D. (1983, 2012). *The Navigator.* Navpress.

God. (n.d.).

Hadidian, A. (1987). *Discipleship: Helping Other Christians Grow.* Moody Publishers.

Hendricks, H. (2007). *Living by the Book.* Moody Publishers.

Henrichsen, W. A. (1988). *Disciples Are Made Not Born.* Wheaton, Ill: Victor Books.

Homer. (1844). *The Iliad.* original unknown: original unknown.

Hull, B. (1983). The Greatest Test of Faith. *The Discipleship Journal.*

Krejcir, D. R. (2002). *What is Discipleship.* Retrieved from Discipleship Tools: http://www.discipleshiptools.org/apps/articles/?articlei d=41167&columnid=4216

McDowell, J. (1986). *More Than a Carpenter.* Living Books.

Newton, J. (1779). Amazing Grace.

Piper, J. (1986). *Desiring God.* Multnomah Books.

Rutherford, D. (2018). *Compelled: The Irresistible Call to Share Your Faith.* christianaudio.com.

Sanders, C. (1952). *An Introduction to Research in English Literary History.* New York: The MacMillan Company.

Smith, T. (2015). Why I Go to Church Even When I Don't Feel Like It. *Relevant Magazine.*

Society of Colonial Wars in the State of Connecticut. (n.d.). Retrieved from Society of Colonial Wars in the State of Connecticut: https://www.colonialwarsct.org/

Velarde, R. (n.d.). *What is the Church?* Retrieved from Focus on the Family: https://focusonthefamily.com/faith/the-study-of-god/why-study-god/what-is-the-church

ABOUT THE AUTHOR

TIM GARLAND

Tim Garland is currently serving as the Lead Teaching Pastor at Grace Fellowship Church in Decatur, Alabama. He is a church planter with the Acts 29 Network. He also is the founder and CEO of Gospel Opportunities Dominican Republic, a discipleship training ministry for Pastors in the Dominican Republic. He has served in youth, college, young married, and singles ministry. Tim was led to Christ and discipled in 1992 and has been discipling men since. He has been happily married to Kelly since 2002. Tim and Kelly have four boys.

LISTEN TO SOME OF TIM'S SERMONS
HTTPS://GRACEDECATUR.COM/RESOURCES/

ACKNOWLEDGMENTS

I would like to thank the faithful men who labored before me and poured into me through the ministry of Campus Outreach: Curtis Tanner, Bryan Brown, Clay Duncan, and Charles Hooper.

After 27 years I could not begin to list all of the men that God has granted me to disciple, nor can I even imagine the impact these men have made on generations to come. There are three impactful stories I will share:

Trace Donahoo – Trace and I met his first year as a student on the University of North Alabama's campus. I challenged him to discipleship. We have labored to make disciples ever since. He has been a part of church plants in England and the United States of America and currently serves as the Lead Teaching Pastor of Immanuel Church in Falkville, Alabama.

Brian Ely – Brian and I met in Panama City Beach, Florida. In the first week of meeting with Brian he trusted in Christ for salvation. I then poured my life into Brian. He graduated and went on staff with the Navigators Ministry, where he is still serving today.

Justin Abercrombie – Justin and I met in Troy, Alabama. Justin was a local banker, and at lunch one day I taught him how to study the Bible. I then met with him over a period of about a year on a regular basis for discipleship. He left banking, went to seminary, became a pastor, received his Doctorate, and is now serving as a seminary professor.

I would also like to thank my loving, enduring wife, Kelly, for putting up with me for the last 17 years. I would like to thank my first disciples now, my four boys—Jay, Ashton, Josh, and Jonathan. I would like to thank my sister, Michelle Segrest, for editing this book for me. I would also like to thank the current and past elders at Grace Fellowship Church for serving with me at a Gospel Centered, Disciple Making Church: Sam Lambert, Jim Yancey, Kelly Meeks, Chase Aldridge, and B. J. Strobel.

Made in United States
Orlando, FL
24 November 2024

54369714R00183